AF822655

Primary Education

A World Bank Policy Paper

The World Bank
Washington, D.C.

1818 H Street, N.W.
Washington, D.C. 20433, U.S.A.

Manufactured in the United States of America
First printing September 1990

Cover design by Walton Rosenquist

ISBN 0-8213-1664-8
ISSN 1014-8124

Contents

Preface

This report was prepared by Marlaine E. Lockheed, task leader, and Deborah Bloch in the Education and Employment Division of the Population and Human Resources Department under the general direction of Ann O. Hamilton and the immediate supervision of Adriaan M. Verspoor. It is based on the evidence presented in a forthcoming book, *Improving Primary Education in Developing Countries,* by Marlaine E. Lockheed and Adriaan M. Verspoor with Deborah Bloch, Pierre Englebert, Bruce Fuller, Elizabeth King, John Middleton, Vicente Paqueo, Alastair Rodd, Ralph Romain, and Michel Welmond. Joanne Capper and Kathryn Dahl edited the manuscript for publication and Cynthia Cristobal provided quick and efficient word processing.

Executive Summary

This report presents policy options for improving the effectiveness of schools in developing countries. The recommendations are based on a broad program of research and evaluation that takes into account various country conditions and experiences. The text focuses on problems common to most developing countries and presents an array of low-cost policy alternatives that have proved useful in a variety of settings.

The material has been organized into six sections. The first describes the importance of primary education and the present failure of education systems to meet their objectives. The second section discusses three areas for improvement: enhancing the learning environment, improving the preparation and motivation of teachers, and strengthening educational management. The third section addresses the need to increase equitable access to schooling. The fourth section covers strategies to strengthen the financial base for primary education. The fifth section discusses international assistance to education, and the sixth section presents implications for World Bank action. A summary of policy recommendations concludes the report.

Primary Education and Development

Education is a cornerstone of economic growth and social development and a principal means of improving the welfare of individuals. Primary education is its foundation. The central purpose of primary education is twofold: to produce a literate and numerate population and to lay the groundwork for further education. However, in many countries in the developing world, education systems have not met their objectives. First, they have been ineffective in teaching students the core skills contained in their national curriculum; second, they have not provided all school-age children, particularly girls, with the opportunity to attend school.[1] As a result, these primary education systems have jeopardized national efforts to build a human capital base for development.

To address these shortcomings, a first priority for primary education is to increase the learning of children in school, so that most children who enroll in school actually complete the primary cycle. A second aim is to provide all school-age children with access to school.

Progess toward these goals depends on efficient use of resources for primary education. In many developing countries, however, there are few opportunities to reallocate resources for greater cost-effectiveness. In the medium term, improving educational effectiveness can yield efficiency savings as students learn more and proceed through the system more rapidly. Although the cost of learning inputs per student is likely to increase, the cost per graduate will go down and more students will complete the primary cycle for the same budget. Capturing these efficiency gains, however, requires significant up-front investments in inputs that enhance learning. Furthermore, these gains alone cannot meet the need for system expansion in most low-income countries.[2] Thus an increase in resources for primary education is essential in these countries. Where insufficient resources are allocated to pursue both objectives simultaneously, the most practical strategy is to concentrate resources on effectively educating a limited number of students. Nonetheless, in countries with growing school-age populations and a large number of children still out of school, such a strategy would be economically and socially detrimental and politically unacceptable.

Most countries recognize that a literate and numerate population is as important as a supportive physical infrastructure and that failure to lay a strong educational foundation will seriously impair a nation's development prospects. Adequate funding of a good-quality primary education system that is widely and equitably available is therefore a critical priority for both national budgets and external aid.

---

1. "School-age children" are generally those six to eleven years old.

2. In this report countries are classified by income according to the *World Development Report 1988* (World Bank 1988). The thirty-nine countries with per capita incomes of less than $450 are classified as low-income economies. The thirty-four lower middle-income economies are those with per capita incomes between $450 and $1,700. The twenty-six upper middle-income economies are those with per capita incomes between $1,700 and $7,425. The seventeen high-income countries are those with per capita incomes greater than $7,425, excluding the high-income oil exporters. Countries that have populations of less than 1 million or that do not report a gross national product (GNP) per capita are not included.

Improving Educational Effectiveness

Improving primary education in developing countries requires effort on at least three fronts: enhancing the learning environment, improving the preparation and motivation of teachers, and strengthening educational management. As countries differ in their problems, so too will they in their responses.

Enhancing the learning environment

Most schooling in developing countries takes place under adverse conditions: in dilapidated school buildings with few educational resources, insufficient instructional hours, poor teaching practices, poorly designed curricula, and classrooms of undernourished and unhealthy children. Given both the impoverished conditions and the severe resource constraints facing poor countries, resources must be used carefully. Theory, research evidence, and experience suggest the following areas in which to invest: (a) *improving the curriculum* to present a coherent, appropriately paced and sequenced instructional program to develop children's literacy, numeracy, and problem-solving skills; (b) *providing instructional materials* in sufficient quantity so that every child has access to textbooks and other reading materials; (c) *increasing instructional time* to ensure a minimum instructional year of 880 hours of class time for core subjects; (d) *improving classroom teaching* through in-service training, interactive radio instruction (IRI), and programmed learning materials; and (e) *increasing students' learning capacity* through preschools targeted at the disadvantaged and through in-school health and nutrition interventions.

Improving the preparation and motivation of teachers

Three critical determinants of effective teaching are knowledge of the subject matter, pedagogical skills, and motivation to teach. All available evidence indicates shortfalls in these areas. To enhance student learning, new teachers need to be better prepared and better motivated than is now the case. Improvements can be accomplished by (a) shifting the general (secondary) education preparation of prospective teachers from teacher training colleges to general secondary schools, (b) shortening preservice teacher training and concentrating it on the development of pedagogical skills, and (c) strengthening teachers' motivation through improved remuneration policies, career opportunities, and working conditions.

However, increasing the general education requirements for primary school teachers could be unaffordable in many low-income developing countries. Civil service pay scales are often based on educational attainment, and teachers are typically included in the civil service. Thus these countries face a predicament: if they raise teachers' educational levels, they incur severe financial obligations they can ill afford. Such countries should consider separating teacher salary scales from civil service scales based on educational attainment. Otherwise, their only option may be to recruit less well-educated but affordable teachers and then invest more in supplementary interventions to sustain student learning.

Strengthening educational management

Measures to improve learning conditions and upgrade teachers will succeed in raising student achievement only where managerial and institutional capacity are strong. Strengthening this capacity generally requires (a) *organizational restructuring* to realign authority and functions between central ministries, intermediate organizations, and schools and to give school managers the necessary authority and resources to manage and improve instruction; (b) *strengthening information systems* for achievement testing, monitoring, research, and the collection of data on enrollment, attendance, inputs, and cost; and (c) *developing managerial competence* by increasing professional opportunities and incentives, clearly defining career paths, and establishing systems to assess performance.

Improving Equitable Access

Despite impressive increases in enrollments during the past two decades, more than two-thirds of all developing countries have yet to achieve their stated goals of universal and equitable access to education.[3] Of the more than 115 million school-age children out of school in developing countries, the vast majority come from one or more of the traditionally disadvantaged groups in society: rural, female, and poor. The three major obstacles to their participation are too few places in schools, too little parental demand for education, and too much discriminatory treatment in school. To extend access to these groups, governments must try to (a) *increase supply* by constructing new schools, renovating existing facilities, recruiting and deploying teachers more effectively, and instituting multiple-shift schooling and multigrade

3. Defined as net enrollment rates of 90 percent or better.

classes; (b) *increase demand* by improving schools, reducing the direct and indirect costs of education, and mobilizing community support; and (c) *equalize treatment of students* by identifying and eliminating discriminatory practices, especially with respect to language of instruction and gender.

Strengthening Financial Support for Primary Education

An infusion of new resources to primary education will be needed to initiate these programs of reform. In most countries, funding for primary education suffers from cost-ineffectiveness, dependency on central government revenues, and inequitable distribution of funds. Redressing these shortcomings will require (a) *using existing primary education resources more efficiently* by shifting expenditures at the margin from inputs that are unrelated to learning to those that enhance student learning and reduce repetition and dropout rates; (b) *mobilizing additional resources for primary education* by shifting government allocations from other sectors to education, devoting more of the education budget to primary education, or raising more revenues locally; and (c) *ensuring equity* of educational inputs everywhere by redistributing national funds according to local needs.

International Assistance to Education

Many poor countries need to supplement their education resources with funds from international donors. Currently, despite high social and economic returns, less than 5 percent of international aid to education ($181 million out of $4.2 billion disbursed annually) is targeted for primary education.[4] To effectively support primary education development in the 1990s, donor agencies must (a) increase the level of aid to primary education; (b) support primary education through subsectoral development programs; and (c) respond with flexibility to unique country conditions. In addition, aid programs need to be coordinated.

Implications for World Bank Action

World Bank lending for primary education began in 1970 and represented about 25 percent of total lending for education between 1981 and 1989. Internationally the Bank is the largest single source of policy advice and external funds for education. It provides about 15 percent of total

---

4. Dollars ($) are constant (1985) U.S. dollars unless otherwise specified.

aid flows to education and about 30 percent of aid flows to primary education. Nonetheless, to respond forcefully to the widespread need for improved primary education, the Bank must expand its lending operations in this area and give special priority to countries considering appropriate programs of reform and development. In particular:

- Higher priority should be given to measures intended to increase children's learning and primary school completion.
- Support for the expansion of access should give explicit priority to girls wherever there are significant gender disparities in enrollment.
- The mobilization and efficient allocation of additional resources for primary education should be a central focus of policy dialogue and lending operations, especially in low-income countries.
- Operations should support long-term primary education development programs.

An expanded Bank effort could be a catalyst for much-needed and broad-based aid flows to the primary education subsector.

Introduction

Education is a cornerstone of economic growth and social development and a principal means of improving the welfare of individuals. It increases the productive capacity of societies and their political, economic, and scientific institutions. It also helps reduce poverty by increasing the value and efficiency of the labor offered by the poor and by mitigating the population, health, and nutritional consequences of poverty. As economies worldwide are transformed by technological advances and new production methods that depend on a well-trained and intellectually flexible labor force, education becomes even more significant.

Primary education has two chief purposes: to produce a literate and numerate population that can deal with problems at home and at work and to serve as a foundation upon which further education is built. However, in many countries in the developing world, education systems have not been able to meet their objectives. First, they have been ineffective in teaching students the core skills contained in their national curriculum; second, they have not provided all school-age children, particularly girls, with the opportunity to attend school. As a result, these primary education systems have jeopardized national efforts to build a human capital base for development.

To address these shortcomings, a first priority for primary education is to increase children's learning in school, so that most who enroll actually master the curriculum and complete the primary cycle. Second, access to school must be provided for all school-age children. Both goals are important. School attendance without learning is meaningless, and development opportunities are missed when a large fraction of the school-age population has no access to schooling.

Developing countries will progress toward these goals only if available resources are allocated to the most cost-effective inputs. In most middle-income countries, education can be significantly improved by reallocating funds within the existing primary education budget. In most low-income countries, however, the scope for such reallocations is limited; additional resources for primary education are essential. Adequate funding of a good-quality primary education system that is widely and equitably available is therefore a critical priority for both national budgets and external aid.

This report presents policy options for improving the effectiveness of primary schools in developing countries. The recommendations are based on a broad program of research and evaluation that takes into account various country conditions and experiences. The text focuses on problems common to most developing countries and presents an array of low-cost policy alternatives that have proved useful in a variety of settings.

The material has been organized into six sections. The first describes the importance of primary education and the present inability of many education systems to meet their objectives. The second section discusses three areas for improvement in order to meet these objectives: enhancing the learning environment, improving the preparation and motivation of teachers, and strengthening educational management. The topic of the third section is increasing equitable access. The fourth section presents strategies for strengthening the financial base for primary education. The fifth section discusses international assistance to education, and the sixth addresses implications for World Bank action. A summary of policy recommendations concludes the report.

1

Primary Education and Development

Most countries recognize the importance of having a literate and numerate population. They acknowledge that a weak educational foundation, like a weak physical infrastructure, will seriously impair a nation's development prospects. Effective primary education thus is a rock-bottom necessity for development.

The Importance of Primary Education

Primary education has direct and positive effects on earnings, farm productivity, and human fertility, as well as intergenerational effects on child health, nutrition, and education. In considering the effects of education on economic productivity, a wide number of studies conclude that investments in primary education yield returns that are typically well above the opportunity cost of capital. One study showed that four years of education increased small-farm productivity by 7 percent across thirteen developing countries and by 10 percent in countries where new agricultural techniques were being introduced. The social effects of education in developing countries are also positive. Women with more than four years of education have 30 percent fewer children than women with no education, and their children have mortality rates only half as high. Children of educated parents are also more likely to enroll in school and to complete more years of school than children of uneducated parents.

The effects of primary education on development are largely a result of the cognitive skills it imparts: literacy, numeracy, and problem-solving skills. At present, because most adults in low-income and lower middle-income countries have not completed primary education (table 1), they largely lack these skills. Increasing the level of education and training of the labor force is thus a central development challenge. A

Table 1. Average Years of Education Completed by Adults in Sixty-five Countries, 1985

Country income level	*Adults age 30–34*	*Adults age 40–44*	*Adults age 50–54*
Low	2.9	2.3	1.7
Lower middle	4.8	3.7	2.7
Upper middle	9.0	7.8	6.9
High	10.1	9.0	8.0

Source: Horn and Arriagada (1986); Komenan (1987).

country's development prospects today hinge much more than even a generation ago on the capacity to acquire, adapt, and advance knowledge. Higher education and training need to rest on a solid foundation, which is essentially the product of the primary education system. In the newly industrialized economies—such as Hong Kong, Israel, Japan, Korea, and Singapore—universal or nearly universal primary enrollment was achieved just before rapid economic growth.

Deficiencies in Primary Education

Poor primary schools compromise the entire system for human capital development. They produce graduates who are poorly prepared for secondary and tertiary education and ill-equipped for lifelong learning. The consequence is an insufficient number of truly educated managers, workers, and parents who can efficiently contribute to development.

The most visible signs of ineffective primary education systems are low primary completion rates and low student achievement. Additionally, in many low-income countries problems of access to schools result in inadequate enrollment, particularly for girls.

Low primary completion rates

In low-income countries fewer than two-thirds of those who enroll in primary school complete the entire cycle. This proportion has been declining in recent years (figure 1). The principal school-related determinants of dropping out are poor learning and repetition. On average, repetition rates in low- and lower middle-income countries are two to five times higher than those in upper middle- and high-income countries, with the highest repetition rates found in the lowest-income countries (table A-1).

Figure 1. Students Reaching Terminal Year of Primary Cycle, 1970-85

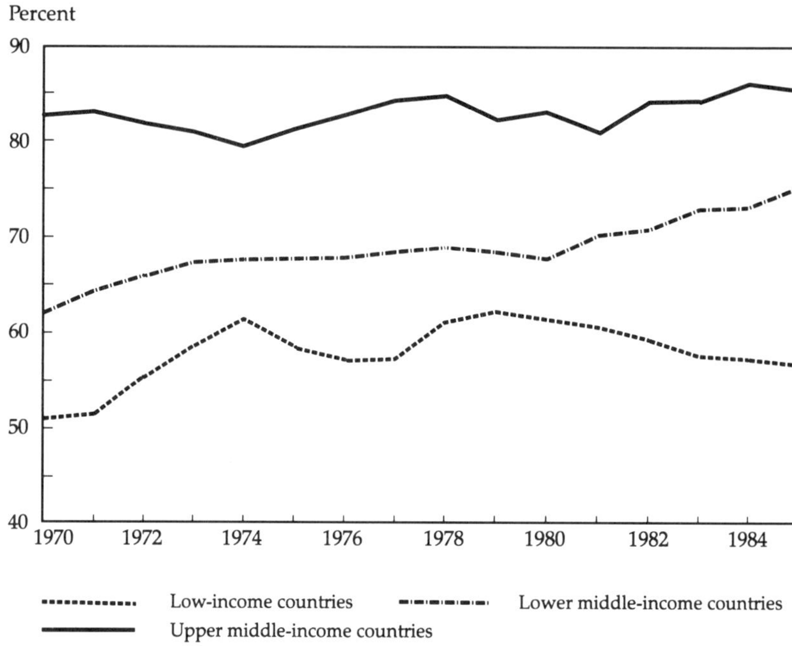

Source: Unesco (1989)

Low student achievement

Even children who complete primary school often have not learned the core skills commonly specified in the national curriculum. Students in low-income countries tend to perform poorly on both national and international measures of cognitive performance in mathematics, science, and reading comprehension (table 2). Performance is poorest on tasks that require students to apply knowledge to new problems.

Inadequate enrollment

Although most middle-income countries have achieved nearly universal primary enrollment, fewer than 75 percent of school-age children in

Table 2. Test Performance of Students in Grades 4–8 in Thirty Countries, for Selected Years, 1970–83
(average percentage of correct answers)

Country income level	*Reading (1970)*	*Arithmetic (1982)*	*Science (1970)*	*Science (1983)*
Low and lower middle	49	39	40	36
Upper middle	55	54	43	53
High	70	52	55	57

Source: Lockheed and Verspoor (forthcoming).

Table 3. Weighted Mean Primary Net Enrollment Ratios in Selected Years, 1965–85

Country income level	*1965*	*1970*	*1975*	*1980*	*1985*
Low[a]	37.6	42.2	48.2	52.6	54.1
China and India	79.6	76.2	76.5	76.2	87.4
Lower middle	63.8	69.1	73.2	85.4	90.3
Upper middle	76.3	80.2	85.0	88.5	90.3
High	94.7	93.4	92.3	91.2	90.6

Note: The net enrollment ratio is the number of children of official school age enrolled in school divided by the number of children of official school age in the population.

a. Excluding China and India.

Source: Lockheed and Verspoor (forthcoming).

low-income countries (54 percent without China and India)[5] are enrolled in primary school (table 3). This is the case even though places are available for 96 percent (67 percent without China and India).[6] In half of low-income countries, fewer than half of school-age children are enrolled, and 68 percent of developing countries have not attained their goal of universal primary enrollment. The majority of those not in school are girls, rural children, and children of the poor.

---

5. Ninety-three percent of school-age children in China and 80 percent of school-age children in India are enrolled in school. Together these two countries account for almost two-thirds of the primary school-age population and 75 percent of primary students in low-income countries.

6. This differences does not reflect excess capacity but rather the fact that many existing places are taken by older children, many of whom are repeating.

2

Improving Educational Effectiveness

Limited educational effectiveness in developing countries results from the failure to provide the minimal inputs necessary for successful learning. In high-income countries a typical primary student goes to a modern, well-equipped school, has 900 hours of learning time and $52 worth of noncapital material inputs per year, studies a well-conceived curriculum, has a teacher with at least sixteen years of education, and enjoys a student-teacher ratio of 20:1. In contrast, students in many low-income countries attend shelterless schools or ones that are poorly constructed and ill-equipped. There are typically only 500 hours of actual learning time annually, $1.70 worth of material inputs per student, and a poorly designed curriculum. Teachers are likely to have less than ten years of education, and classes may consist of more than 50 children, many of whom are chronically undernourished, parasite-ridden, and hungry.

Enhancing the Learning Environment

Given both the impoverished conditions and the severe resource constraints facing poor countries, it is critical to concentrate resources on interventions that improve learning, are cost-effective, and can be widely implemented. Theory, research evidence, and experience suggest five principal areas in which to invest: the curriculum, learning materials, instructional time, classroom teaching, and students' learning capacity. Developing countries instead have invested primarily in two other inputs thought to be prerequisites for access: school buildings and teachers. The consequence is that children enroll in school but they learn little and do not complete the primary cycle.

Improving students' performance requires reallocating resources to ensure adequate levels of the five inputs necessary for learning. Figure 2 provides an overview of the process that links these inputs with

Figure 2. A Model of Effective Schooling

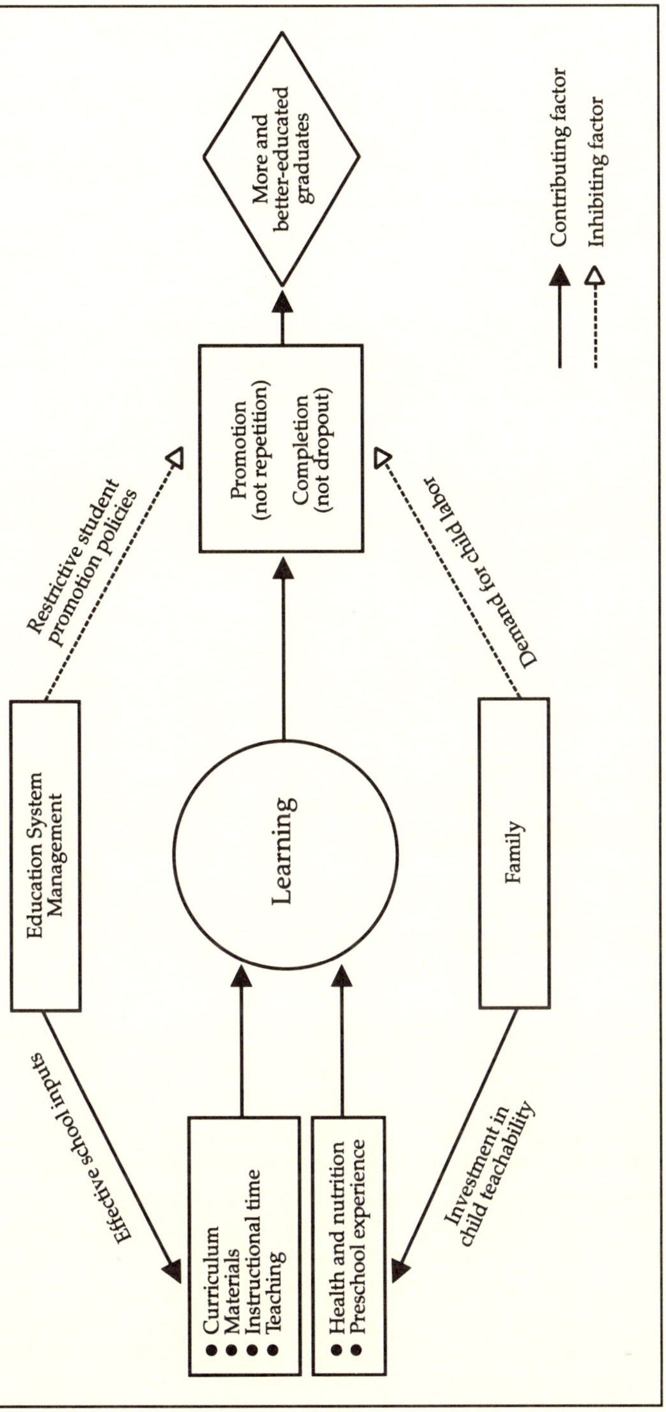

children's learning and completing primary school. Children's learning is a function of family background and school inputs. Family background characteristics that enhance children's teachability are investments in health, nutrition, and preschool experience. The school-related inputs discussed in this section—curriculum, learning materials, instructional time, and teaching methods—are those that have been found to have the most significant effect on student learning.

Provision and effective use of adequate amounts of these inputs are the responsibility of education management at all levels. Learning contributes to children's staying in school and being promoted on time, while demands for child labor outside the classroom and restrictive school promotion policies detract from attendance and advancement. When learning is increased, therefore, and attendance and promotion are not inhibited by exogenous factors, children remain in school for more of the primary years, move through the system more rapidly, and complete the primary cycle in greater numbers. The result is more and better-educated primary school graduates.

The curriculum

Primary school curricula are remarkably similar worldwide. Regardless of level of economic or educational development, countries teach the same subjects and accord them the same relative importance. Approximately 35 percent of available instructional time is devoted to the acquisition of language skills and 18 percent of time to mathematics. Science, social studies, and the arts are given equal weight, about half that of mathematics and one-fourth that of language (table A-2). In developing countries, however, instructional time for language is often divided between a national or local language and a nonindigenous official language, which may lower levels of achievement in either language.

Despite commonalities in official curricula, there are great disparities in what is in fact taught. The actual curriculum in many developing countries is poor in both scope and sequence of instructional material. A recent study of the reading and mathematics curricula in fifteen developing countries found that expectations for student achievement in the earliest grades were inappropriately high and that steps from one concept to the next were very large with few intermediate steps. Furthermore, textbooks—the major, if not only, definition of the curriculum in most developing country schools—also suffer from factual inaccuracies, inappropriate illustrations, poor writing, and a lack of material to develop higher-order thinking skills such as problem solving, critical thinking, and reasoning.

Most curriculum reforms have concentrated on redefining the courses to be taught and the number of hours officially allocated to each. Generally these changes have been ineffective. Successful curriculum reform efforts must tackle the more difficult issue of preparing a coherent, appropriately paced and sequenced instructional program and developing effective instructional materials.

Learning materials

Instructional materials are key ingredients in learning. They provide information, organize the presentation of information, offer students opportunities to use what they have learned, and—in the case of tests and quizzes—allow teachers to assess student learning. The learning materials known to enhance student achievement most significantly are textbooks and teacher guides.

BOOKS AND LIBRARIES. Over the past decade, researchers have found that the availability of books has a consistently positive effect on student achievement in developing countries. For example, on tests of mathematics achievement in Nicaragua, students who were given textbooks scored about one-third of a standard deviation higher than students without textbooks. Similarly, in Brazil, second- and fourth-grade students who received textbooks scored significantly higher on tests of mathematics and Portuguese than students without textbooks. Likewise, in Fiji, provision of classroom libraries led to improved test scores (box 1).

However, in many developing countries primary school students either lack books altogether or are required to share books with other students. For example, in the Philippines before a massive investment in textbooks, the student-to-textbook ratio was 10:1; in the Dominican Republic, fewer than 20 percent of eighth-grade students in public schools have mathematics textbooks; in the Central African Republic, there is one French text for every ten to twenty students.

TEACHER GUIDES. Teacher guides that are well integrated with the textbook or with other instructional materials can have a positive impact on student achievement. Particularly effective are guides that include (a) information on both what to teach and how to teach it; (b) diagnostic tests to help teachers monitor student learning and modify lessons based on test results; (c) strategies for classroom management; and (d) suggested class activities.

Box 1. The "Book Flood" Experiment in Fiji

In 1980, grade 4 and 5 classes in eight rural schools in Fiji were inundated with a wide range of high-interest, illustrated storybooks in English. Each grade 4 and 5 teacher received 250 books. Half the "Book Flood" teachers were trained to use the Shared Book method, whereby the teacher spends several days discussing the book, the pictures, and the title and reading aloud while the children listen. The other half of the teachers merely encouraged children to read silently for thirty minutes each day. A control group of similar children were taught English using a conventional approach without any reading books.

Students were tested before the Book Flood began, again after eight months of the program, and again one year later. Both Book Flood groups showed much greater improvement than the control group. In the first eight months, the Shared Book group and the Silent Reading group had each improved their reading levels by 15 months, while the control group had shown only 6.5 months' gain. After nearly two years with the enriched reading program, the Book Flood groups had increased their growth even more, and the effects had spread to writing, formal grammar, and other subjects. The effects also persisted on the national examinations, in which the pass rate was twice as high for Book Flood students (73%) as for students in conventional rural schools (37%).

Source: Elley and Mangubhai (1983).

OTHER MATERIALS. Evidence is less clear about the impact of other basic instructional aids (such as chalk and blackboards), although common sense suggests that their availability is important. While properly implemented computer-based learning programs can be effective, their present costs make widespread introduction infeasible for most education systems in developing countries, particularly in rural areas where the necessary supporting infrastructure is typically unavailable. In general, country priorities should focus on the provision of pedagogically sound, culturally relevant, and physically durable books for all students and curriculum guides for teachers.

Instructional time

Research from a number of countries has shown that the amount of time available for academic studies is consistently related to how much children learn in school. In general, the more time teachers spend actually teaching, the more students learn. While classroom instruction is valuable for all students, it is especially important for poor students, whose out-of-school time and opportunities for learning are limited.

Three factors determine the annual number of hours allotted to study any subject in school: the length of the official school year in hours, the proportion of these hours assigned to the subject, and the amount of time lost through school closings, teacher absences, student absences, and miscellaneous interruptions.

Worldwide, the official academic year for primary grades 1–6 averages 880 instructional hours, or 180 days, with slightly fewer hours in lower-income countries than in higher-income countries (table A-3). In some developing countries, the academic year is substantially shorter than average (for example, 610 hours in Ghana); in others it is longer (1,070 hours in Morocco). Since curricular emphasis at the primary level is relatively consistent across countries, with approximately 35 percent of available time spent on literacy and 18 percent spent on numeracy, the official number of hours available for instruction of these subjects is similar for both industrial and developing countries.

However, time loss for unscheduled school closings, teacher absences, disruptions, and inclement weather is much greater in developing countries. For example, in Haiti the school year in 1984 had 162 days—18 short of the international standard—but it was made significantly shorter by unofficial closings and delayed openings. The school day often began late, teachers frequently were absent on Tuesday and Friday (market days), and forty-eight public holidays were celebrated instead of the twenty-eight holidays built into the school year. Teacher absences due to administrative procedures are also common in developing countries. For example, many teachers must travel considerable distances to be paid, while others are assigned to schools far from their homes; both situations contribute to teacher absences and reduced instructional time.

A popular but costly strategy to increase learning time is reducing class size. Small classes are often considered indicators of educational quality. But the main benefit of small classes is to increase the student-teacher contact time. This happens only in very small classes. Teachers' classroom interaction with individual students is fairly minimal until classes are twenty students or fewer. While reducing classes to this size could boost achievement, in most countries such reduction is prohibitively expensive. A more promising and more effective strategy for increasing learning time is to set and maintain standards for instructional time. This can be done in two ways: increasing the amount of official time allocated to learning and increasing the amount of actual time spent on learning.

INCREASING OFFICIAL TIME. In countries where the school year comprises fewer instructional hours than international practice (about 880 hours), it can be lengthened. In many cases this is an attractive alternative, as it permits full coverage of the conventional primary curriculum. Where double shifts necessitate a school year of fewer than 880 hours or where the introduction of a second language limits curriculum options, maintenance of minimum instructional time (about twenty hours weekly) in core subjects, especially reading and mathematics, may need to take priority over covering a wide range of subjects.

MAINTAINING OFFICIAL TIME. Maintaining instructional time requires administrative and/or parental interventions to ensure that (a) schools are open during official hours and children are in attendance, (b) teachers are present and teaching during the official instructional periods, (c) temporary distractions, such as administrative or visitor interruptions, are avoided, and (d) appropriate arrangements are made for continuing instruction under routine inclement weather conditions such as rain.

Classroom teaching

The quality of teaching plays a critical role in students' achievement. Effective teaching strategies may differ by subject and grade; that is, strategies that are appropriate for children in preschool and the early elementary grades may not work for older children, and vice versa. Effective teaching involves, at a minimum: (a) presenting material in a rational and orderly fashion, pacing the class to the students' level and taking into account individual differences; (b) providing students with opportunities to practice and apply what they have learned; (c) letting students know what is expected of them; and (d) monitoring and evaluating student performance in such a way that students can learn from their own mistakes.

Much teaching in developing countries is characterized by teaching practices that are not conducive to student learning, such as heavy reliance on teacher lectures with few opportunities for student questions and participation, student memorization of material rather than application of knowledge, and little ongoing monitoring and assessment of student learning through homework and classroom tests. For example, a study in Nepal found that 78 percent of fifth-grade science instruction was lecturing and less than 7 percent was student participation. In Thailand 54 percent of fifth-grade mathematics instruction consisted of teacher lectures, explanations, or demonstrations; another 30 percent of the time was spent on written work; only 4 percent of the time was used for oral work of any kind. In Botswana students listened to the teacher's lecture during 54 percent of the observed instructional time and spent another 43 percent of the time on oral recitation.

Three resources can improve classroom teaching: in-service training for teachers, interactive radio instruction for children, and programmed learning materials.

IN-SERVICE TRAINING. Most in-service teacher training programs emphasize pedagogical practices. Those that are most effective employ continuous efforts rather than "one-shot" courses. In Bangladesh, for example, recurrent school-based in-service teacher training concentrated on topics such as practical methods of teaching major subjects, ways to adapt the curriculum to the social and physical environment of the student, understanding how children develop and learn, methods of evaluating teaching and learning, management of classrooms, and parent-teacher and community relations. In-service training programs in India, Nigeria, and Thailand have provided incumbent teachers with a new repertoire of pedagogical skills that focus on more participatory teaching behaviors.

In-service training can be carried out through distance education programs (correspondence courses, often supported by radio). This form of training is cost-effective and particularly useful for improving teachers' subject matter knowledge. In Latin America two-thirds of all post-secondary distance education institutions provide teacher training; in Africa teacher education has proved to be the most successful use of distance education. One study found that distance teacher training in Tanzania was not only more effective than an equivalent conventional residential program, it was also four times cheaper per graduate. Similarly, a distance teacher training program in Brazil (described in box 2) was found to be six times more cost-effective than traditional, residential teacher training methods.

INTERACTIVE RADIO INSTRUCTION (IRI). Interactive radio pays close attention to the correct order and pacing of instruction, which is broadcast directly into classrooms. When teachers lack sufficient subject matter knowledge to instruct students correctly in a particular area, IRI can be an effective supplemental teaching tool. Studies in five countries showed that IRI students learned more mathematics and English than children taught these subjects in conventional classrooms. IRI is also one of the most cost-effective educational interventions. Once lessons have been developed, they can be transmitted to thousands of new students every year at minimal cost.

Box 2. Teacher Training through Distance Education in Brazil

The Logos II distance education teacher training program in Brazil is a self-paced learning program that teaches both subject matter and pedagogy. All students are uncertified primary school teachers who are currently employed. The curriculum consists of a number of modules, or short courses on specific topics, presented in pamphlets. The topics range from mastering the curriculum to techniques for teaching. Students study the pamphlets at home and go to learning centers to be tested on the modules. Other student activities at the learning centers include microteaching sessions, special tutoring in more difficult topics, socializing opportunities, and study groups. The entire program takes from thirty to fifty weeks to complete, after which students take a certification examination.

Source: Oliveira and Orivel (1981).

PROGRAMMED MATERIALS. A third way to improve teaching by incumbent teachers is to use programmed materials. Like IRI, programmed materials focus on the systematic application of various principles of instructional development and design. They provide step-by-step scripts for teachers and instructional materials for children to use individually or in groups. They have been used successfully in primary schools in Indonesia, Liberia, the Philippines, and Thailand.

Students' learning capacity

Children's capacity for learning is largely determined by their health and nutritional status and by their prior learning. There is ample evidence that preschool nutritional and stimulus deprivations are associated with deficits in cognitive development. Children in developing countries are likely to be malnourished and to have had little exposure to learning materials before entering school. In-school nutrition and health programs can improve cognitive performance, and preschool educational programs can compensate for academic deprivations in the home environment.

IN-SCHOOL NUTRITIONAL SUPPLEMENTATION AND HEALTH SCREENING. There are only a few valid studies of the effects of school feeding programs on enrollment and achievement. Although the results are encouraging, the available analyses fail to show a clear relationship between school lunch programs and educational results. School breakfasts or snacks may be more cost-effective in alleviating short-term hunger and its adverse impact on learning. To counteract micronutritional deficiencies, supplements of iodine, iron, and vitamin A are highly cost-effective, and deworming is an inexpensive approach to dealing with parasites. Visual and auditory screening can be conducted with simple eye charts and "whisper" tests at negligible cost.

PRESCHOOLS. Research in both industrial and developing countries demonstrates that preschool experience, including attendance at Koranic schools, has positive effects that are often sustained for several years. Targeted preschool programs, aimed at families with low incomes, have been particularly effective. Publicly financed preschool experience for all children is not feasible for most developing countries, but private and community-supported preschools—including those supported largely by nongovernmental organizations (NGOs)—should be encouraged.

Improving the Preparation and Motivation of Teachers

Three critical determinants of effective teaching are knowledge of the subject matter, pedagogical skills, and motivation to teach. All available evidence indicates shortfalls in these areas.

Knowledge of the subject matter

A key factor in teaching effectiveness is the general academic preparation of the teacher, which can take place either before or during teacher training. In most developing countries, prospective primary teachers have only about nine years of general education and represent the least able of their classmates. In countries with high rates of population growth, rapid expansion of the primary education system has led to a reduction in the amount of general education needed for entry into teacher training programs. In Nigeria, for example, only five years of primary education were required in 1981.

Such inadequate preparation results in trainees who lack the intellectual and academic background to acquire adequate pedagogical skills. Therefore, teacher training programs have been obliged to devote valuable time to academic remediation. Students in teacher training colleges spend as much as 80 percent of their time on general secondary subjects.

Providing general secondary education in teacher training colleges is quite expensive, averaging seven times the annual per-student cost in conventional secondary schools (table A-4). The higher direct costs reflect the tendency of teacher training programs to be both residential and remunerative; trainees are paid stipends for food and lodging, and they earn salaries while in training. Significant savings can be gained by requiring prospective teachers to obtain their secondary education in general secondary schools.

Pedagogical skills

Pedagogical proficiency is a second key determinant of effective teaching. Yet because teacher training programs devote so much time to general secondary education, little attention is paid to pedagogy. Moreover, the pedagogical course work often concentrates on broad theoretical issues rather than specific instructional strategies (table A-5). A shorter teacher training program, focused on the development of pedagogical skills, would be more cost-effective than present programs. A shorter program assumes, however, that prospective teachers have already completed general secondary education. The shorter program could provide prospective teachers with opportunities for practice teaching under the supervision of a master teacher. Practice teaching helps prospective teachers master pedagogical skills and also prepares them to cope with unexpected events in the classroom.

Teacher motivation

Low teacher morale leads to high rates of teacher absenteeism and attrition. Teacher absenteeism reduces student learning time, while teacher attrition increases the costs of teacher training. Low morale undermines even the most conscientious and capable teacher's enthusiasm for teaching. The causes are low salaries, poor working conditions, insufficient career advancement opportunities, and/or weak support services.

SALARIES. Salaries and benefits are important motivating factors in any profession. In developing countries, teacher salaries and emoluments account for as much as 95 percent of recurrent government expenditures on primary schools. Teacher salaries in some countries are high relative to manufacturing wages, but often they are lower (table A-6). In many developing countries, average teacher salaries have been eroded significantly over the past two decades. A recent World Bank study found that per-teacher spending has fallen 30 percent on average among West African countries and 20 percent among East African countries since 1970. Between 1980 and 1985, real teacher earnings declined 20 percent in Francophone Africa and 13 percent in eastern and southern Africa. In

Somalia the average teacher salary is about half the average cost of living—even following a recent doubling of wages (in current terms); teachers now earn the equivalent of $6 per month, or 25 percent of GNP per capita annually.

When salaries are this low, teachers are likely to supplement their incomes by other pursuits, a practice that increases teacher absenteeism. Surveys in Indonesia, Liberia, and Somalia all show substantial proportions of primary teachers holding second and sometimes third wage-earning jobs.

WORKING CONDITIONS. In general, conditions within the classroom are poor and instructional materials are in short supply. Facilities are inadequate and poorly maintained. In many countries there is a perennial shortage of classrooms, and in urban areas often more than fifty-five students are crammed into rooms built for half that number. These conditions demoralize teachers and discourage their professional commitment.

CAREER ADVANCEMENT OPPORTUNITIES. In most developing countries, teachers' career and salary advancement seldom depends on performance. Salaries tend to be tied to civil service pay scales, with raises awarded on the basis of certificates and length of service. Thus there are few incentives for teachers to perform well. Career ladders linked to redesigned salary scales can have a positive impact on teacher motivation. They can offer teachers the opportunity to develop new skills and accept new challenges; they can provide good role models by placing experienced teachers in positions to influence younger teachers; and they can facilitate teacher involvement and responsibility at the school level. As a result, they can motivate teacher performance.

SUPPORT SERVICES. The lack of supervisory and support services for teachers also adversely affects teacher motivation. For example, late payment of salaries was found to be a major disincentive in Haiti, Liberia, and Yemen. Moreover, teachers absent themselves from school to travel to the administrative offices to collect their payments. Similarly, the lack of regular supervision discourages the adoption of improved teaching practices and encourages absenteeism.

To strengthen teacher motivation, comprehensive strategies are needed that pay attention to both salaries and nonsalary benefits. Competitive salary schedules must be established, along with opportunities for advancement and incentives for performance, such as grants for innovative teaching projects. An adequate salary structure will be effective, however, only in conjunction with working conditions and professional support at the school level that allow teachers to adopt demonstrably effective instructional strategies.

Dilemma for low- and lower middle-income countries

The education sector is the single largest wage employer in the world, with the primary education sector employing more than 19 million teachers worldwide, including 8.7 million in low-income countries. Teacher emoluments account for over 90 percent of recurrent government expenditures on primary education (table A-7). Projected growth in school-age populations, plus teacher attrition, will require preparation and employment of hundreds of thousands of additional primary school teachers annually just to maintain current levels of enrollment.

Achieving 100 percent gross enrollment by the year 2000 would mean training about 7.9 million new teachers in low-income countries and 4.5 million new teachers in middle-income countries (table A-8). For low-income countries anticipating economic growth of only 3–4 percent a year, the latter scenario implies a 6 percent increase in the teacher supply and concomitant increases in expenditures for teacher training and salaries.

To avoid perpetuating poor teaching, improvements must be made in teachers' general education background, pedagogical skills, and motivation. However, raising the general education prerequisites for teacher training can have significant budgetary consequences. This is because teacher salary scales typically parallel civil service salary scales and are often based on formal certification and years of experience. Entry-level salaries are generally higher for primary school teachers with secondary school certificates (and some teacher training) than for teachers without a secondary certificate. For example, in Rwanda the salaries of "instituteurs" (highest certification level) are more than twice those of "instituteur-auxiliaires" (lowest certification level), and in Côte d'Ivoire each additional year of general education is associated with a 17 percent increase in teacher salary.

To raise the general education requirements for primary school teachers and retain existing linkages between general education attainment (qualifications) and entry-level salaries could be unaffordable in many developing countries. This is particularly true where average primary teacher salaries are already many times manufacturing wages and where the expected number of teachers will rise significantly to accommodate a growing school-age population. If a country cannot separate teacher salary scales from equivalent civil service scales based on educational attainment and if it cannot let education requirements rise with no resultant increase in salaries, the only option may be to recruit less well-educated (but affordable) teachers. Such a decision would then require investments in supplementary interventions to motivate teachers, improve their classroom teaching, and lower attrition. These interventions might include interactive radio instruction, programmed learning, and distance education programs to upgrade teacher qualifications (so that salary increases would be deferred into the future).

Strengthening Educational Management

Effective schools require effective school management and well-developed national and intermediary organizations to provide the necessary leadership and resources. The most successful reform efforts have targeted the school as a whole rather than students, teachers, curriculum, or administrators in isolation. Governments must create a context that promotes competence at the school level. While each country has to develop its own strategy, strengthening the managerial and institutional capacity of the system may require organizational restructuring, strengthening information systems, and developing managerial competence.

Organizational restructuring

Organizational structure is the context within which management takes place. Structure imparts authority, responsibility, and control and helps determine how efficiently and effectively the system functions. Some education systems are highly centralized: financing and authority are concentrated at the national or, in large countries, the state level, with districts and schools carrying out a centrally mandated and financed program of schooling. Other systems are relatively decentralized, with authority to mobilize and use resources resting at the district, municipality, or state level. Whether education systems are centralized or decentralized (and there are advantages and disadvantages to both, as described in box 3), the system should be organized so that decisionmaking authority and resources are properly matched to support the development and operation of effective schools.

Administrative weaknesses at the central level generally arise when managers' time is consumed by operational tasks at the expense of strategic matters. The proper functions of central-level administration include broad policy planning, developing new curricula and materials, designing policy implementation strategies, designing and monitoring standards of performance, providing financial resources and technical expertise, and obtaining and distributing educational materials. However, central-level managers are often hampered in the execution of their jobs because of cumbersome or outdated procedures, weak coordination among ministries, vaguely defined responsibilities, and haphazard policy formulation processes.

At intermediate levels, education offices tend to be poorly financed and inadequately staffed. Their principal responsibility is to provide professional support and technical assistance to individual schools. However, these functions are often poorly executed because of inadequate resources. Inspection and supervision of schools require regular school visits, which in turn require sufficient staff and vehicles. In Senegal, for example, school visits were limited by lack of transportation: there were only twenty-eight vehicles to be used by more than 600 staff in forty-one regional directorates. In Honduras only 53 percent of the schools were visited in 1986, each only once.

At the school level, the management effectiveness of principals is often jeopardized by limitations on their authority to control the delivery of instruction in the school. Yet virtually every line of inquiry about school

Box 3. Centralized Versus Decentralized Control

There are advantages and disadvantages to both centralized and decentralized education systems. Centralized control can be effective in countries where a strong sense of nationhood has not yet developed and in countries characterized by political and economic stability, good infrastructure, and a relatively homogeneous context for schooling. Centralization may also be more efficient for achieving scale economies or national consistency in activities such as textbook production, curriculum development, monitoring, and teacher training. This is particularly beneficial in environments with scarce financial and managerial resources. Most important, even when local governments provide education more efficiently than the central government, central government inputs (and financing) are necessary to ensure equity and to set standards for appropriate service levels and outcomes.

Highly centralized control, however, can lead to bottlenecks of information and resource flows and limit the ability of schools to respond to local needs. When decisionmaking authority is concentrated at the top, central-level staff spend large amounts of their time on tasks that could be more efficiently carried out by intermediate and school-level managers.

Source: Hanson (1986); Winkler (1989).

improvement identifies the principal as a critical factor. For example, a recent study of primary school effectiveness in Burundi showed a strong positive relationship between the frequency of the school director's classroom visits and student test scores.

The principal's responsibilities are multifaceted and complex. They include community and parent relations, supervision of teachers, maintenance of facilities and equipment, reporting and record keeping, and, in small schools, teaching. Yet principals are significantly constrained by chronic shortages of materials, clerical support, operating funds, and resources for staff development. Additionally, principals have little control over the hiring or disciplining of their teachers because teachers are often appointed, assigned, and evaluated centrally. One goal of decentralization is to give school managers the authority necessary to manage and improve instruction and to mobilize local resources.

An appropriately structured educational organization gives managers at all levels adequate authority and resources to do their jobs effectively. The education organization in many countries needs to be restructured, with authority and functions realigned between central ministries, intermediary organizations, and schools. This implies (a) limiting the task of central-level agencies to strategic planning, standard setting, and performance monitoring, (b) providing effective intermediate-level supervisory and support services, and (c) encouraging local school improvement initiatives, stimulating community involvement, and delegating responsibility for instructional improvement to school managers.

Improving intermediate-level supervision and support is critically important to the success of sectoral improvement programs. Strategies that have proved effective include creating an additional layer of supervisory staff (such as assistant education officers in Bangladesh and learning coordinators in Pakistan), establishing cluster systems (as in India, Myanmar, Nigeria, Papua New Guinea, Sri Lanka, Thailand, and many Latin American countries), and providing vehicles and gas to encourage regular school visits by intermediate-level staff.

Strengthening information systems

Good management depends upon the systematic collection and application of information relevant to improving schools. Information must be useful for, and made available to, decisionmakers at all levels. However, few countries have yet developed the information systems necessary for educational policymaking. Further work is needed in three areas: testing, monitoring, and research.

Box 4. Establishing Accountability through Achievement Testing in Thailand

In response to the absence of administrative control over the thousands of primary schools in Thailand, the Office of the National Primary Education Commission (ONPEC) initiated national testing for sixth-grade students in 1984. The program began with a pilot test in 15 percent of the districts in every province. The following year the program expanded to sample of students in every district, and it has continued that way ever since.

From 1984 to 1988, ONPEC invited all provincial educational directors to annual meetings where mean scores, standard deviations, and rankings based on scores and degree of improvement were announced. Provinces with outstanding scores and those that had achieved dramatic gains made presentations on the strategies they used. Directors from provinces ranking in the bottom third met privately with the Secretary-General and other key staff from ONPEC to discuss their specific problems, plans for improving test scores, and special needs that might justify additional resources.

Provinces then began to rank districts and to meet regularly with the heads of the district offices to discuss progress. Districts in turn started their own testing systems and began to rank schools and individual classroom teachers according to the performance of their students on tests.

The resulting higher test scores show that schools, principals, and classroom teachers have indeed begun to pay greater attention to academic learning. Except for 1987, achievement scores and the percentage of students who satisfactorily master a given area have increased substantially, as indicated in the table below. And although it is not clear why scores dropped in 1987, they were still significantly higher than in 1984.

Table B-1. Student Achievement on National Sixth-Grade Examinations, 1984–87

Subject	*1984*	*1985*	*1986*	*1987*
		Mean scores		
Thai language	49.1	56.8	58.4	56.3
Mathematics	33.1	36.5	47.8	46.2
		Percentage attaining satisfactory scores		
Thai language	47	69	76	64
Mathematics	11	18	41	40

Source: Thailand, Ministry of Education (1987); Wheeler and others (1989).

ASSESSING ACHIEVEMENT. A capacity for continual assessment of student achievement is essential to improving the quality of education. Assessment of student learning is most effective when conducted separately from the examinations students must take for admission to higher levels of education. A national program for ongoing assessment of student learning is needed to evaluate the impact of policies and programs and to permit reliable reporting of student learning on a regional basis. This will enable central staff to monitor the progress of regions over time, both to ensure quality control and to identify regions (education districts, states, provinces, and so on) that may need additional help. The initiation of a national test for sixth-grade students in Thailand has led to increased accountability of teachers, principals, schools, and districts and consequently has increased student achievement, as described in box 4.

A central testing agency, adequately staffed to offer extension services to schools and districts, can provide important support for school improvement programs. By developing a variety of tests based on the national curriculum and by providing technical support and training to local educators, the testing agency can help them evaluate student learning and the effects of school-improvement initiatives.

BUILDING MONITORING SYSTEMS. Stronger monitoring systems are needed to capture basic statistical information on teacher qualifications and deployment, student characteristics, school attendance, dropout, repetition, and costs. Where data can be developed and reported from the school and aggregated at the intermediate level, it becomes possible to compare student achievement across regions, enabling regions to monitor indicators of school quality. To be useful, these data must be assembled and reported routinely and in a timely manner.

DEVELOPING RESEARCH CAPACITY. Economic and educational research will be needed to complement routine information gathered through testing and monitoring systems. Among the issues that need to be addressed are the effectiveness of learning materials, the impact of training on teacher and principal performance, the educational outcomes and equity effects of school improvement strategies, the effectiveness of supervision, the cost-effectiveness of various interventions, and the impact of alternative instructional practices. It is also important to identify and disseminate examples of good practice and local innovation among schools. Publicizing successful school-based initiatives not only provides models for consideration in other schools but also reinforces and rewards local accomplishment.

Combining these functions (testing, monitoring, and research) into a strong information system depends on comprehensive and long-term institutional development strategies. Experience suggests that these functions are best located in specialized institutions (for example, the National Examinations Council in Kenya, the Education Development Institute in Korea, and the National Examinations Board in Malawi).

Developing managerial competence

Weaknesses in institutional management have been identified in almost all developing countries as rapid expansion of education systems has increased the need for managers and administrators. At high levels, key positions are often filled by people who have little experience in educational policy and planning, often because they are rapidly promoted or appointed to fill vacancies created by frequent turnover and expansion. Institutes that train education administrators are few and likely to be handicapped by shortages of staff, teaching materials, and funds. The result is that many ministries are staffed with underqualified, inexperienced individuals who are unable to carry out their managerial responsibilities.

The absence of effective managers is also evident at intermediate and school levels. Intermediate staff are often appointed on the basis of seniority or political relations, and they often lack up-to-date expertise in curriculum development and pedagogical methods. At the school level, principals are selected from the ranks of teachers on the basis of seniority, and they receive little, if any, systematic training.

Strengthening managerial capability at all levels will require substantial resources and a long-term perspective. The dual problems of lack of skilled managers and low morale need to be tackled by providing systematic staff development programs, increasing professional opportunities and incentives, clearly defining career paths, and establishing systems for assessing performance. Training should be linked to clear long-term strategies for organizational development. To maintain managerial competence, countries eventually must develop specialized institutes for training educational managers at all levels (such as the Unit for Education Administration in Indonesia, the National Institute of Education Management in Malaysia, and Management Training for Education Personnel in Tanzania).

3

Improving Equitable Access

Despite impressive increases in enrollments during the past two decades, many governments have yet to achieve their stated goals of universal and equitable access to education. While middle-income countries can provide primary education to virtually all school-age children, in low-income countries (other than China and India) the availability of primary school places is limited. Even if all existing places were filled solely by six- to eleven-year-olds, only about 50 percent of those now out of school could be accommodated (table A-9).

Characteristics of out-of-school children

Of the 115–145 million school-age children out of school in developing countries, the vast majority come from one or more of the traditionally disadvantaged groups in society: rural, female, and poor.[7]

RURAL CHILDREN. Urban children are more likely to enroll in and complete primary school than rural children. Fewer than 50 percent of rural children in most countries, and as few as 10 percent in many countries, complete more than four grades of school. Major impediments to education in rural areas include lack of schools, lack of resources (including teachers, materials, facilities, and equipment), lack of reinforcement for education in the local environment, differences between the language of instruction and local languages, household and farm chores that com-

---

7. Differences in definitions of primary school-age populations make it difficult to obtain a firm figure for the out-of-school group. Estimates of six- to eleven-year-olds not in school in developing countries range from 115 million to 145 million; this includes China, where six year-old children are not expected to be in school.

pete for time in the child's schedule; and incomplete primary schools, offering fewer than the official number of primary grades.

FEMALES. Although the gap between the numbers of girls and boys in primary school has narrowed since 1960, the enrollment of girls continues to lag in many countries. The gender disparity in some countries is particularly stark. In northern Yemen there are 90 percent fewer girls enrolled in primary school than boys; in Nepal, 57 percent fewer; and in Guinea Bissau, 41 percent fewer. The most significant obstacles to female education include lack of schools for girls when education is sex-segregated, reluctance among female teachers to work in isolated rural areas or in urban slums, perceived irrelevance of primary school curricula to women's employment possibilities, demand for girls' household labor, restrictions placed upon girls' physical mobility, and, among older girls, increased likelihood of pregnancy and/or preparation for marriage.

POOR CHILDREN. In all countries, children of poor families are less apt to enroll in school and more apt to drop out than children of better-off families. One study in India and Nepal found that student enrollment in the richest families exceeded that of the poorest by 50–100 percent. Families incur both direct and indirect costs of education. Direct costs include school fees, uniforms, school supplies, and transportation. Families also incur opportunity costs in the form of foregone household labor or earned income of children in school. In Egypt the cost of schooling was the reason most often cited by parents for not sending their children to school.

Strategies aimed at enrolling more out-of-school children include increasing the supply of school places, increasing the demand for education, and equalizing the treatment of those in school.

Increasing supply

Extending access to children who are currently out of school often requires increasing the supply of school places. There are a number of strategies that can be used.

SCHOOLS AND FACILITIES. Building more schools is an obvious and necessary response to the inadequate number of school places, provided that schools are located within children's walking distance. Distance from school is a critical factor in school attendance, especially for girls. For example, in Egypt the enrollment of girls who lived 2 kilometers from school was 8 percent lower than that of girls who lived within

1 kilometer from school; enrollment for boys who lived farther away was 4 percent lower. Before undertaking the expense of building complete schools, governments (or communities) should consider expanding existing schools or using existing buildings such as churches and community centers. Another improvement that can increase enrollment, particularly of girls, is building sanitary facilities in schools.

TEACHER RECRUITMENT AND DEPLOYMENT. Teacher shortages are common in rural areas, and incentives may be needed to encourage teachers to work in isolated areas. Some incentives include the provision of boarding facilities, increased training, or even additional pay. Increasing the supply of female teachers, in particular, is an effective way to increase girls' school attendance in a number of countries. In rural India, communities that recruited female secondary school graduates to teach classes experienced significant declines in the dropout rate of children, especially girls.

PRIVATE SCHOOLS. Primary education in most developing countries is publicly provided; an average of 90 percent of all primary students are enrolled in public schools. However, tightening fiscal constraints have limited the ability of the public sector in many countries to expand public education. One option is allowing private schools to meet excess demand. To do this, countries must lift restrictions on the provision of private schooling. However, policymakers must carefully consider the extent to which private primary schools may attract students from wealthy families and consequently reduce national commitment to public schooling.

MULTIPLE SHIFTS. Multiple shifts have the dual advantage of increasing enrollments and reducing per-student costs. By organizing separate class sessions (for example, in the morning and afternoon) and by having teachers share facilities, two or three times as many students can be accommodated and savings can be realized on capital and teacher costs. If multiple shifts shorten the school day, the school year can be made longer to compensate.

MULTIGRADE CLASSES. Multigrade classes, in which one teacher teaches several grades, are an effective way to increase access in rural communities. Multigrade teaching addresses two problems: uneconomically small classes and incomplete schools. Combined with appropriately designed instructional materials and teacher training, multigrade teaching has led to higher student achievement in several countries, notably Colombia and Indonesia.

SINGLE-SEX SCHOOLS. In countries where schooling is sex-segregated, providing schools for girls is necessary to increase female enrollment and attendance. Various mechanisms exist for establishing single-sex schools; these include constructing separate buildings for boys and girls, using the same facilities at different times for boys and girls, and holding single-sex classes in coeducational schools.

NONTRADITIONAL SCHOOLING. In general, formal primary schooling is the preferred means of teaching basic literacy and numeracy skills. However, because many children who belong to disadvantaged groups live and work in areas where schools are either absent or unsuitable, other schemes of providing education may be necessary. A key condition for the success of nontraditional schools is to ensure equivalency with formal primary schools; otherwise, they will be rejected as inferior.

Increasing demand for schooling

To increase enrollment, encouraging perennially out-of-school groups to seek education is at least as important as increasing the supply of school places. Strategies generally have to include improving primary schools, reducing direct costs to families, reducing indirect costs to families, and mobilizing community support and public information.

IMPROVING PRIMARY SCHOOLS. Increasing demand for education depends largely on persuading parents that education is valuable. Thus one of the most significant ways to increase demand is to improve the effectiveness of education, so that parents see greater benefits in sending their children to school.

REDUCING DIRECT COSTS TO FAMILIES. In some countries the direct costs of primary school attendance (for fees, transportation, uniforms, and instructional materials) can reach 20 percent of a family's income. Efforts to reduce the cost of education for rural families have been undertaken in several countries. These efforts have included reduction or elimination of school fees, provision of instructional materials and uniforms, free or subsidized transportation, direct subsidies to households for the purchase of materials and uniforms, school meal programs, and scholarships.

Several countries, including Bangladesh and China, have also provided cost incentives specifically to encourage girls' attendance. In Bangladesh 50 percent of the primary scholarships given at the end of Class 5 are reserved for girls. In rural, mountainous, and minority areas in China, a package of incentives including boarding schools, books, stationery, medical allowances, educational guidance, and parental education has increased participation rates of girls to over 90 percent.

REDUCING INDIRECT COSTS TO FAMILIES. Reducing indirect costs is often as important as reducing direct costs. Strategies to reduce indirect costs include changing the school calendar to accommodate seasonal demands for child labor, providing child care for younger siblings, and instituting labor-saving technologies. In Bangladesh flexible scheduling is one of several key strategies used to increase the school participation of girls and rural children. In China built-in childcare facilities at places of employment have successfully improved female enrollment in urban areas. Establishing preschools close to primary schools has also helped increase girls' attendance in primary schools.

MOBILIZING COMMUNITY SUPPORT. When parents are active in the educational process, it is more likely that their children will attend school. Many countries have adopted a variety of measures to garner community support for education, ranging from village peasant associations in Ethiopia to mass consciousness-raising campaigns in China. Public information campaigns in a number of countries have successfully addressed misconceptions about the purpose and value of schooling.

Equalizing treatment

Redressing discriminatory treatment requires a genuine commitment to understanding the sources of unequal treatment and to instituting corrective measures. In some cases discrimination is easy to identify and remedy. For example, when boys' schools receive more educational resources than girls' schools, or urban schools more than rural schools, the obvious solution is to reallocate resources. When texts portray certain population groups (females, minorities) in negative ways, they should be rewritten.

Perhaps the most difficult form of discrimination to address is that of language of instruction. The language policy debate is long-standing. On one side are advocates of first-language instruction, who argue that literacy skills acquired in one language are transferable to other languages and that developing these skills is easiest in the child's home language. On the other side are those who argue that not only are children who are taught in a local language at a disadvantage for further educational opportunities, but spending time developing literacy skills in their first language reduces the time available for learning an official or national language.

Determining a sound language policy will necessarily be heavily influenced by the unique economic, cultural, political, and linguistic factors in each country. However, the balance of available evidence indicates that, under the circumstances in many developing countries, it is most effective to begin with the home language as the medium of instruction and later switch to the necessary second language. Box 5 describes an effective bilingual education program in Guatemala.

Box 5. Improving Equity through Bilingual Education in Guatemala

Historically, language was a major reason for the limited access of the indigenous Mayan population to educational opportunities in Guatemala. While most children from this population spoke a Mayan language—there are over 200—the language of instruction was Spanish. In a pilot bilingual program introduced in 1980 in forty rural schools, children were taught in one of four major Mayan languages for the first three primary grades; then instruction was shifted to Spanish.

As is often the case with bilingual programs, at the outset there was some parental resistance: parents feared their children would receive an inferior education and would not learn Spanish. These concerns were overcome when parents saw the improvements in children's achievement and their mastery of Spanish along with the indigenous language. In 1986 the bilingual program (PRONEBI) expanded to 400 schools; by 1990 the number of schools is expected to reach 800. In fact, national law now requires bilingual education in rural communities where a Mayan language is spoken.

Source: Chesterfield and Seelye (1986).

4

Strengthening Financial Support for Primary Education

The combined demands of increased learning, better management, better teachers, and expanded access imply a need for substantial resources. (Table A-10 summarizes the cost implications of the recommendations presented here.) In the medium term, improving educational effectiveness can yield efficiency savings as students learn more and proceed through the system more rapidly. While the cost of learning inputs per student is likely to increase, the cost per graduate will go down, and more students will complete the primary cycle for the same budget.

Capturing these efficiency gains, however, requires significant upfront investments in inputs that enhance learning. Furthermore, these gains cannot fully fund system expansion in most low-income countries. Where insufficient resources are allocated to pursue both objectives simultaneously, the most practical strategy is to concentrate resources on effectively educating a limited number of students. However, in countries with growing school-age populations and a large number of children still out of school, such a strategy would be economically and socially detrimental and politically unacceptable.

The Need for Increased Funding

Many developing countries have underinvested in education in general and primary education in particular, and all social sector budgets have suffered from the adverse economic conditions and austerity measures of the late 1970s and early 1980s. Moreover, by any indicator, resources available per student are low and have declined in low-income countries.

The school-age population as a proportion of total population in low-income countries is 75 percent higher than that in middle- or high-income countries. However, since 1965 public expenditures on education, expressed as a percentage of GNP, have been lower in low-income than in middle- or high-income countries. Moreover, they have remained relatively constant at about 3 percent, while steadily increasing in middle- and high-income countries to 4–6 percent (table A-11).

In real terms, recurrent public expenditures per primary pupil have declined in low-income countries while increasing steadily in middle- and high-income countries. Between 1965 and 1985, per-student expenditures dropped from $41 to $31 (stable from 1980) in low-income countries; they increased from $73 to $102 in lower middle-income countries, from $194 to $297 in upper middle-income countries, and from $825 to $1,551 in high-income countries (table A-12).

In 1965 recurrent per-student expenditures amounted to 20 percent of GNP per capita in low-income countries; by 1980, this figure had fallen to under 12 percent. In lower middle-income countries there was little change over time, while in both upper middle- and high-income countries the effort increased significantly, from 10.6 percent to 12.5 percent and from 11.7 percent to 17.6 percent respectively (table A-13). To a large extent, reduction in public spending for education in the poorest countries was a consequence of economic adversity and the need to reduce inflation, domestic consumption, and public expenditures.

Improving primary education will require that the spending declines in low-income countries be reversed and that additional resources be committed. While the primary responsibility for child rearing and education must remain with parents, society has legitimate interests in the education and socialization of children. There are two reasons that make substantial government financing imperative. First, the optimal amount of human capital investment will not be reached if parents must pay the full cost of educating their children, because parents do not take into account the external benefits of education when making their private cost-benefit calculations. Second, since primary education is the single most powerful accepted tool for economic and social mobility, concern for the welfare of the poor demands that education be financed so as to provide access regardless of ability to pay.

Raising learning to minimum acceptable levels for the majority of those presently in school requires raising nonsalary recurrent expenditures per student. The magnitude of the resources needed depends upon the particular country, its present level of provision, and the costs of specific inputs. However, figures for instructional materials alone can serve as a general indicator. The average central government expenditure for educational materials per student in 1985 was about $1 in low-income countries, about $2 in lower middle-income countries, and

Table 4. Central Government Expenditures on Teaching Materials

Country income level	*Average expenditures per primary student*[a] *(1985 dollars)*	*Number of countries*
Low	0.8	18
Lower middle	1.8	18
Upper middle	5.5	15
High	52.4	9

a. Average is weighted by country-level primary student enrollments.
Source: Lockheed and Verspoor (forthcoming).

about $6 in upper middle-income countries (table 4). To raise low- and lower middle-income countries to the level of upper middle-income countries would therefore require spending an additional $5 and $4 per student, respectively.

Increasing annual per-student expenditures by $5 in low-income countries (excluding China and India) and $4 in lower middle-income countries could cost as much as $1 billion a year in the next ten years.[8] For low-income countries, this $5 increase would raise the primary education budget by 20 percent and the total education budget by 10 percent. For lower middle-income countries, the effect of this budget increase would be much less pronounced, representing a 4 percent increase in the primary education budget and a 2 percent increase in the total education budget.

These increases for essential material inputs are substantial, particularly for low-income countries, and not likely to be fully fundable from local sources. Even more resources would be required to provide other important nonsalary inputs such as in-service teacher training and supervision. Although considerable savings may ultimately result from benefits associated with increasing learning inputs per student, capturing the savings is likely to take at least five to ten years.

In addition to spending more on nonsalary inputs, many countries need to find the resources to increase expenditure for teacher salaries and to expand access. In low-income countries, savings from increased efficiency will be insufficient to meet these demands. The challenge, therefore, is finding additional resources to begin the process and sustain the commitment.

---

8. An additional $1 billion would be required for China and India.

Mobilizing Resources for Primary Education

Education financing typically suffers from three related shortcomings:

- Cost-ineffectiveness. Resources are often allocated to inputs that have only a weak relationship to educational productivity, while inputs that enhance learning are underfunded.
- *Dependency.* The national resource base of education is narrow and overly dependent upon central government general revenues. Little attention is given to alternative sources of funding, including private sources.
- *Inequity.* In many countries a considerable proportion of public finance for education goes to middle- and upper-income families.

Financial strengthening of primary education should try to redress these shortcomings by (a) making reallocations within the primary education subsector, (b) expanding and improving funding for primary education, and (c) promoting more equitable allocation of public resources.

Reallocations within the primary subsector

Research indicates three major opportunities to make better use of existing primary education funds. Savings could be had with no negative effect on student learning by increasing the student-teacher ratio (to 40–50:1), building schools with low-cost (often local) materials, and shortening the length of preservice teacher training.

As discussed earlier, schools in developing countries have few resources other than teachers. However, since the average student-teacher ratio in most developing countries is less than 40:1, increasing this ratio could free resources for other inputs (tables A-14 and A-15).[9] The feasibility of this strategy in any given country will depend on existing student-teacher ratios and the dispersion of the school-age population. Reallocations are most feasible where student-teacher ratios are less than 40:1 (such as China); resources then could be shifted from teachers to other necessary inputs. In the few countries that have student-teacher ratios greater than 50:1 (such as Burkina Faso), increasing the student-teacher ratio is unlikely to be feasible or desirable. Alternative organiza-

---

9. Fifty-four percent of low-income countries, 79 percent of lower middle-income countries, and 96 percent of upper middle-income countries reported student-teacher ratios of 40:1 or less in 1985. Only nine low-income countries (23 percent) had average ratios greater than 50:1.

tional arrangements may help, and usually additional resources will be required.

Another way to reduce costs with little negative effect on achievement is to minimize the investment costs of school construction. A first strategy is to build schools with local materials. Although there is evidence that children in schools with electricity and water learn more than those in schools without these facilities, other improvements in construction have shown little impact on student achievement. Holding classes in locally available buildings, such as churches or mosques, and renovating existing schools instead of building new ones are two other ways to reduce construction costs and save resources.

Finally, the costs of teacher training can be significantly reduced by shifting the general secondary education component of teacher training to general secondary schools and reducing the length of teacher training accordingly. Savings obtained from this strategy could be made available for recurrent in-service teacher training, thereby increasing primary students' achievement.

Where funds cannot be reallocated within the primary subsector, other savings may still be possible. In countries where repetition is common and largely determined by deficiencies in learning, the initial investment of incremental resources can be regained from future savings. The median repetition rate for primary school students is 16 percent in low-income countries, with some countries reporting repetition rates over 30 percent. Empirical evidence shows that under conditions of high repetition and dropout, investments in inputs that promote learning can actually yield economic returns. When relevant inputs are added, students learn more, move through the grades more rapidly, and complete school sooner. The costs of educating a graduate are thus reduced, and resources are then freed for other educational purposes. Box 6 takes the case of Brazil as an example of the economic yields that can be gained by reducing repetition.

Additional resources

Whatever efficiency gains are possible within the primary education subsector, the fact remains that primary education in most low-income countries is underfunded. Additional resources are needed to make initial investments in cost-effective inputs, to provide facilities for growing school-age populations, and to extend access to out-of-school populations. Governments, therefore, may need to increase the priority of primary education in the allocation of the education budget. Since the potential social contribution of primary education is high and the risk of

Box 6. Efficiency Gains in Northeast Brazil

With financial assistance from the World Bank, the Brazilian government undertook in 1980 a program of massive educational investment in rural schools in the northeast, the poorest region in the country. A six-year evaluation showed increased student learning, which in turn reduced student repetition. The result was a significant cost savings, as fewer resources were consumed by repeaters. For example, investing $1 per student in writing materials and textbooks shortened the average length of time for a student to progress from second to fourth grade by 0.13 years. Since the annual cost per student was $30, this $1 investment reduced the total cost of producing a fourth-grade student by $4.03 (table B-2).

Table B-2. Cost and Savings for Selected Educational Investments in Brazil, in the 1980s
(dollars)

		Savings per dollar invested[a]			
		Rural northeast		*Brazil*	
Input	*Cost per student*	*Low-income schools*	*All schools*	*Low-income schools*	*All schools*
Textbooks and writing materials	3.41	4.03	3.12	2.86	0.81
Buildings, furniture, and equipment	5.45	2.39	1.84	1.69	0.47
In-service distance teacher training	1.84	1.88	1.45	1.33	0.37

a. The estimated savings based on years saved, valued at $30 per student year, in producing a fourth-grade student.
Source: Harbison and Hanushek (forthcoming).

private underinvestment substantial, governments should avoid rationing access to primary schools on the basis of ability to pay. Public subsidies may have to rise faster for primary education than for education at other levels. The case for such a strategy is strongest when one or more of the following conditions are met: primary enrollment rates are low; the social rate of return for primary education is substantially higher than that for postprimary levels; public subsidy of education is not targeted at the neediest; the beneficiaries of postprimary education are predominantly children of upper-income families; and/or the share of postprimary education in the total government budget is relatively high. Cost recovery is more appropriate at higher levels than for primary education.

Additional resources for primary education could be obtained in two other ways. First, governments could shift allocations from other sectors to education. Second, they could diversify the sources of funding for primary education by instituting new taxes and strengthening local finance. Significant sums have been generated at the local level through school-based organizations such as parent-teacher associations. These groups generate resources by collecting school fees, soliciting voluntary contributions, and organizing social fund-raising events. Table A-16 illustrates the various kinds of contributions that local communities in Zambia have made to primary schools.

Ensuring equity

Some ways in which education is financed—including reliance on local financing for primary education—can contribute to the inequities in the provision of education described earlier. The task of equalizing educational opportunity is not easy and can be accomplished only with the political commitment of the central government. One major step is to use central government funds to complement locally generated resources. The poorest communities may be financially overburdened and unable to spend more on education, but wealthier communities can bear a larger share of education costs, freeing central government resources for greater assistance to impoverished communities.

Governments can establish differential criteria for the allocation of national funds for education. The strategies will vary according to the country's objectives and institutional constraints. For example, using a system of targeting and indexing, the central government can select a group of poor communities for special attention. The government's per-student allocation to primary schools in these areas can then be linked and equated to the average expenditure (from all sources) of a sample of schools in nonpoor communities. Management information systems can assist in monitoring the results of these and other financing actions.

5

International Assistance to Education

The deep need for improved primary education in developing countries, and the substantial costs involved, point to the need for increased international assistance.

A Profile of Education Aid

During the 1980s, 9.2 percent of all bilateral and multilateral aid to development was targeted at education, for an average annual allocation of $4.2 billion. More than 95 percent of this assistance was directed to secondary and tertiary levels of education, while primary education remained generally neglected. Between 1981 and 1986, *all* international aid disbursed to primary education amounted to only $181.3 million annually and represented only 4.3 percent of the annual total aid to all levels of education for the same time. Most aid to primary education was provided to low- and lower middle-income countries. Low-income countries received about 33 percent of all aid, and lower middle-income countries 57 percent. Not only were aid flows to primary education small during the 1980s, they declined in low- and lower middle-income countries in real terms (figure 3).

Moreover, the majority of aid to primary education was not allocated to those inputs that have been found to be most cost-effective. For all recipient countries, only 4.8 percent of total aid to primary education between 1981 and 1986 went to pedagogical inputs such as textbooks and instructional materials, while 30 percent supported infrastructure (buildings, furniture, and equipment). Teacher training received only 7 percent of total aid; the training and support of administrative staff received 2 percent (8 percent if combined with unspecified administrative support); and curriculum reforms received 4.5 percent. The neglect of support for pedagogical materials is particularly notable in low-income countries, where buildings, furniture, equipment, food, and scholarship expenditures accounted for 59 percent of all aid. In lower middle-income countries, this percentage amounted to 42.7 percent (table A-17).

Priorities for Donor Support

The current challenges facing educational development and the necessity to build strong, sustainable, and good-quality primary education suggest that past patterns of donor aid may no longer be appropriate. To effectively support primary education development in the 1990s, donor agencies will need to (a) increase allocations to primary education, particularly for quality improvement and, in some low-income countries, for capacity expansion; (b) provide broad support to primary

Figure 3. International Donor Aid Flows to Primary Education, 1981-86

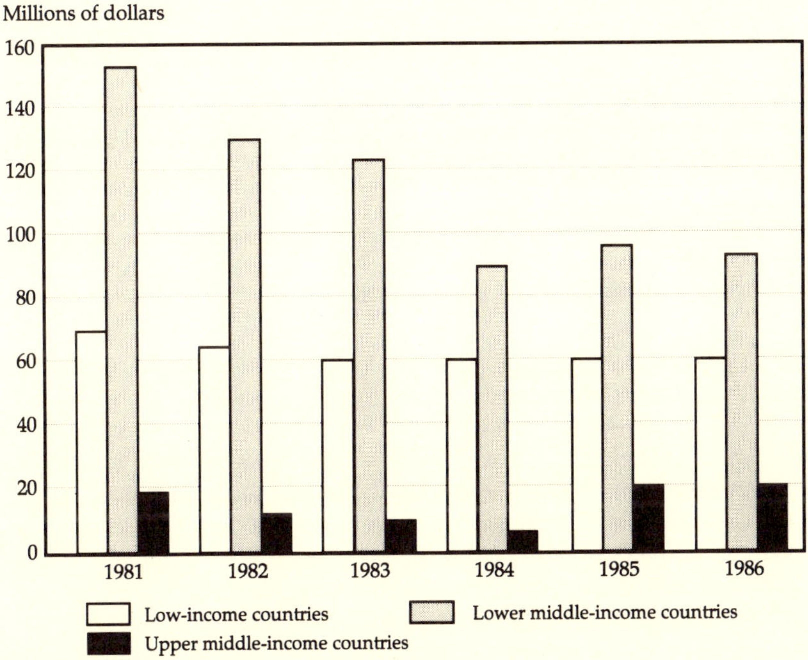

Note: These figures represent three-year running averages.
Source: World Bank (1988); IREDU (1989).

education development programs; and (c) respond flexibly to country-specific needs and priorities.

However, effective donor assistance will depend not only on the degree to which aid is increased but also on the extent to which it is coordinated and used. For optimal efficiency, aid programs must be mutually supportive and reinforcing, and focused upon improving the policy and institutional framework for educational development.

Increasing the level of aid

The low level of aid to primary education and the urgent need to spur educational progress make a compelling case for increased aid to primary education. Although in many countries investments in learning materials, teacher training, and management will—over time—result in yields from greater efficiency, start-up costs will often be considerable and external financial support will be essential to bridge the gap between feasible and essential outlays.

Increased aid, however, needs to be targeted more effectively than it has been in the past. Although many low-income countries will continue to require external support in their efforts to educate more students, the first funding priority for expanded external aid programs should be improving the conditions for and management of learning. In middle-income countries donor support may be less critical, but in these countries in particular, support should shift from buildings and furniture to better pedagogical materials and teaching methods. In almost all countries, targeting aid more effectively, particularly within subsectoral programs, is critical to the revitalization of primary education systems.

Supporting primary education development programs

For the proposed expansion of external assistance to be effective, it is important to support primary education through broad subsectoral development programs, in addition to making specific project investments. In the World Bank's experience, successful sectoral and subsectoral development programs require at least three elements: in-depth analysis of sector issues, concentration on a few policy and institutional objectives, and a persistent commitment to these objectives over time.

Subsectoral development programs usually include both recurrent and investment expenditures, span up to a decade, define specific investment priorities, and specify a policy framework. Depending on the country's conditions and donor preferences, external financing can be commingled with national resources or targeted toward specific activities. At regular intervals progress is reviewed and necessary adjustments carried out.

The analytical background work, the definition of investment priorities, the development of the policy framework, and program implementation are best handled by national specialists. Whenever possible, specific investments should be appraised by a national agency according to agreed criteria. Staff of donor agencies should increasingly play a facilitating and analytical support role, instead of the traditional technical expert role. To pave the way for recipient countries to take more responsibility for designing and implementing primary education development programs, donors should stand ready to aggressively support the development and strengthening of national institutions for research, planning, and implementation management.

Responding with flexibility

Priorities will differ among countries. While textbooks might be of the utmost urgency in some countries, other countries may have a greater need to upgrade their physical plant or improve school management. Each country will have to analyze its own situation, define its own priorities, and prepare its own national program for primary education development and reform. Consequently, donors will have to be flexible in their support of education development programs.

6

Implications for World Bank Action

Primary education lies at the heart of all efforts to develop human resources. In addition to its well-established and direct positive effect on productivity, it has strong effects on health, nutrition, and population and is the foundation for advanced education and training. Primary education is therefore central to the Bank's efforts to improve the productivity and quality of life of poor people and to build the human capital necessary for sustained development in the 1990s.

Bank Support for Primary Education

The World Bank began lending for education in 1963 and for primary education in 1970. Since then, the Bank has increased its lending for primary education steadily to average more than 25 percent of its total education lending in recent years (table A-18). The Bank has committed more than $2 billion altogether in assistance for primary education, and it is now the largest single donor agency, having disbursed about 27 percent of all international aid to primary education during 1981–86.

Initially Bank lending focused on the provision of buildings and furniture; in the late 1970s the emphasis shifted to textbooks. Recent lending has become more policy-oriented, addressing sectorwide constraints in the policy framework for primary education development in borrowing countries. To a large degree this reflects growing concern for the cost and financing implications associated with structural adjustment in the poorest developing countries.

In several countries with strong education institutions, primary education development has been supported through sector investment loans. Sector investment loans differ from conventional loans in that they support a time-slice or key elements of a longer-term sectoral investment program rather than discrete projects. By relying on the borrower for the detailed preparation and appraisal of specific investment proposals, sector lending has enabled Bank staff to focus on crucial policy and institutional issues and on the transfer of knowledge and experience.

Priorities for the 1990s

Mobilizing additional external funding for primary education is a high development priority for the 1990s. The Bank should demonstrate its support for primary education by expanding its lending operations in this area. Special priority should be given to those countries that have embarked upon or are considering programs of reform and development that focus on the most cost-effective inputs and institutional strengthening.

The findings of policy analysis and research presented in the preceding sections suggest that, to help countries respond effectively to the challenges of primary education development, Bank lending should evolve in four ways:

- Higher priority should be given to measures intended to increase children's learning and primary school completion.
- Support for the expansion of access should give explicit priority to girls wherever there are significant gender disparities in enrollment.
- The mobilization and efficient allocation of additional resources for primary education should be a central focus of policy dialogue and lending operations, especially in low-income countries.
- Operations should provide funding to support long-term primary development programs.

These evolving priorities in Bank lending should be discussed with policymakers and planners in borrowing countries in the course of the Bank's economic and sector dialogues.

Learning and school completion

Bank lending for primary education has traditionally emphasized financing for primary school construction, preservice teacher training, and curriculum development. In recent years support for the provision of educational materials and in-service teacher training has increased significantly. This trend needs to be accelerated. In addition, Bank loans for primary education should systematically consider the need to:

- Introduce systems for the regular collection and reporting of data on student achievement and other key performance indicators.
- Support reforms in the organization of initial and in-service teacher training, the structure of the teaching profession, and teacher remuneration and promotion policies.
- Establish or strengthen programs aimed at training headmasters and other education administrators.
- Assist preschool education targeted at low-income areas through provision of support services, instructional materials, and other nonsalary recurrent costs in accordance with Bank policy.
- Integrate nutrition and health interventions into primary school improvement programs and preschool interventions.

Girls' education

In many countries gender disparities in enrollments remain significant. Experience shows that increasing school places does not automatically result in a higher proportion of girls attending school. Bank lending should, therefore, aggressively support increasing education opportunities for girls wherever they are underenrolled. In these countries Bank loans should:

- Make schools more accessible to girls. This involves ensuring that schools are located within easy reach of girls (even when this requires more and smaller buildings), rapidly expanding the number of girls' schools where primary education is sex-segregated, and providing for the privacy and safety of girls and female teachers.
- Support the recruitment and training of female teachers for at least 50 percent of the classrooms to be constructed.
- Consider the provision of incentives and the elimination of disincentives for girls' attendance and completion of the primary cycle.
- Include programs to educate parents about the social and economic role of females and the value and importance of girls' education.
- Recommend scheduling classes more flexibly in terms of hours, days, and seasons.

Resource mobilization and allocation

In many low-income countries the level of public funding for primary education has declined to a point where effective teaching and learning can no longer be expected to take place. Redressing this situation will usually require a combination of measures to mobilize additional domestic and external resources and to allocate them to the most cost-effective inputs. Specifically the Bank should:

- Review, in country economic and sector analyses, the adequacy of expenditures for primary education, their distribution among salary and nonsalary recurrent costs, and opportunities for redirecting funds from other sectors to education and funds from other education subsectors to primary education.
- Encourage the reallocation of available resources to cost-effective, quality-enhancing inputs.
- Actively support the diversification of funding sources for primary education, including the mobilization of local and community resources.
- Ensure that equity considerations are taken into account in the allocation of public subsidies to different levels of education and to regions.

Long-term support

Past Bank investments in primary education have been most successful in their support for the expansion of access. Support for quality improvement has been emphasized more in recent years. It has been most successful where the Bank has entered into a long-term collaborative relationship with the government and assisted it to address subsector-wide policy issues at the national level, strengthen the institutional capacity system-wide, and implement educational improvements at the school level.

Broad-based and expanded support to increase educational effectiveness will therefore usually need to (a) be designed as part of longer-term national education development programs, (b) be conceived and implemented by capable national agencies, and (c) give clear priority to strengthening analytical capacity and management in developing countries.

Well-designed subsectoral development programs will also allow borrowers to coordinate more effectively the inputs of various external donor agencies. Wherever possible, the Bank should integrate its lending operations and analytical work in the frame of such coordinated programs.

Summary of Recommendations

The overall recommendations of this report focus on improving the effectiveness of schools, increasing equitable access, and finding the resources necessary to support those objectives. Two final recommendations are addressed specifically to the World Bank.

Recommendations to Improve Educational Effectiveness

- Emphasize learning. Developing countries need to increase the number of children who acquire the skills specified in their nation's curriculum and who successfully complete the primary cycle. To this end, countries must emphasize students' *learning* as the key policy objective. While enrollment expansion, especially for girls, is of critical importance in several countries, a prerequisite is that the education process achieve its goal of educating.
- Invest in what works cost-effectively. To improve learning, countries need to invest in educational interventions that work, are cost-effective, and can be widely implemented. Resources within the primary education subsector should be rechanneled from inputs unrelated to learning into those that enhance learning. Minimum levels of the five necessary inputs must be ensured: a well-structured curriculum; plentiful textbooks and teacher guides; twenty hours a week of instruction in core subjects; good teaching (through regular on-site in-service training for teachers and through interactive radio instruction and/or programmed materials for children); and selected nutrition and health interventions.
- Improve the next generation of teachers. Children's learning is strongly affected by the general education, pedagogical skills, and motivation of their teachers. Improvements in these areas can be accomplished by (a) shifting the general education preparation of

prospective teachers to general secondary schools or distance education programs, (b) shortening formal preservice teacher training sharply and concentrating it on the development of pedagogical skills, and (c) strengthening teachers' motivation through improved remuneration policies, career opportunities, and working conditions.

- Improve management. School improvement cannot take place without an adequate administrative and management structure. Countries need to invest resources in strengthening the institutional capacity of their education systems. Strategies can include (a) restructuring the educational organization to give managers at all levels the authority and resources to do their jobs effectively, (b) strengthening information systems by developing national assessments of learning achievement, building monitoring systems, and developing research capacity, and (c) developing managerial competence through systematic staff development programs, increased professional opportunities, and clearly defined career paths.

Recommendations to Expand Equitable Access

- Increase the supply of school places through multiple shifts, low-cost construction of schools, and larger classes.
- Increase parental demand for education.
- Eliminate discriminatory treatment of children in school.

Recommendations for Financing Improvements

- Increase national resources for primary education.
- Increase donor aid. To effectively support primary education development in the 1990s, donor agencies should (a) increase allocations to primary education, particularly for quality-enhancing inputs, (b) provide their support in the framework of subsectoral development programs where appropriate, and (c) respond with flexibility to different country conditions.

Recommendations to the World Bank

- Expand support for primary education programs emphasizing student learning.
- Design lending operations in the context of long-term national subsectoral development programs.

Appendix

Table A-1. Median Repetition Rates of Primary Students, for Selected Years, 1965–85
(percent)

Country income level	*1965*	*1970*	*1975*	*1980*	*1985*
Low	21.7	20.9	17.0	15.6	17.0
Lower middle	19.5	15.8	11.4	11.6	10.6
Upper middle	10.3	11.4	9.3	6.5	8.5
High	6.5	4.6	3.1	2.2	2.0

Source: Lockheed and Verspoor (forthcoming).

Table A-2. Curriculum Time Devoted to Major Content Areas in 90 Countries, in the 1980s
(percent)

Curriculum content	*Low-income countries*	*Lower middle-income countries*	*Upper middle-income countries*	*High-income countries*
Language	37	34	36	34
Mathematics	18	17	18	19
Science	7	9	8	6
Social Studies	8	10	9	9
Moral Education	5	6	4	5
Music and Art	9	8	11	13
Physical Education	7	6	7	9
Hygiene	1	2	2	1
Vocational Subjects	6	7	3	1
Other	3	3	2	3

Source: Benavot and Kamens (1989).

Table A-3. Official Instruction Time by Subject in 110 Countries, in the 1980s
(average annual hours)

Country income level	*Total*	*Language*	*Mathematics*
Low	870	322	157
Lower middle	862	293	147
Upper middle	896	323	161
High	914	311	174

Source: Benavot and Kamens (1989), updated tables.

Table A-4. Teacher Training Cost in Relation to General Secondary Education Cost in Selected Countries
(current domestic currencies)

Country	*Unit cost of teacher training as a multiple of general secondary education cost*
Cape Verde	9.07
Central African Republic	9.07
China	8.51
Dominican Republic	8.68
Gambia	10.43
Guinea-Bissau	6.55
Haiti	6.31
Liberia	10.12
Madagascar	8.60
Mali	12.82
Mauritania	4.61
Pakistan	25.53
Tonga	34.67
Average ratio (27 countries)	7.06

Source: Lockheed and Verspoor (forthcoming).

Table A-5. Primary Teacher Training Programs in Selected Countries

Country	Length of program (years)	Curriculum content: General education (percent)	Curriculum content: Theory (percent)	Curriculum content: Practice teaching (percent)
Ecuador	2	39	40	21
Egypt	5	61	19	20
India	2	40	40	20
Lesotho	3	—	—	33
Malaysia	2	73	8	19
Morocco	1	80	10	10
Somalia	2	86	11	3
Thailand	2	84	13	3
Yemen (northern)	5	80	15	5

— Not available.
Source: Lockheed and Verspoor (forthcoming).

Table A-6. Average Primary Teacher's Salary in Selected Countries

Country income level	Year	Amount (1985 dollars)	Ratio to non-agricultural wage	Ratio to GNP per capita
Low				
Burundi	1985	1,704.00	1.03	7.2
Ghana	1986	787.90	1.09	2.0
India	1986	1,041.90	1.35	3.6
Kenya	1984	1,295.40	0.86	4.6
Malawi	1986	849.70	1.28	5.8
Tanzania	1979	1,072.00	1.36	3.0
Zambia	1982	2,483.90	0.93	6.1
Lower middle				
Chile	1981	2,845.70	0.74	2.0
Costa Rica	1986	4,760.30	1.87	3.2
Guatemala	1979	2,489.60	2.68	1.7
Honduras	1982	3,307.30	0.81	4.2
Mauritius	1986	1,161.50	1.43	0.9
Peru	1985	1,145.40	1.81	1.3
Thailand	1986	1,861.60	1.25	2.3
Zimbabwe	1984	3,549.90	1.04	6.6
Upper middle				
Greece	1985	7,219.60	1.53	2.2
Mexico	1986	1,733.30	0.77	0.9
Portugal	1985	5,055.70	1.95	2.6
Venezuela	1984	5,125.10	0.53	1.5

Source: Computed from ILO (1988); Lockheed and Verspoor (forthcoming).

Table A-7. Expenditures on Teacher Salaries in Relation to Government Recurrent Expenditures on Primary Education, in the 1980s

Country income level	*Median percentage spent on teacher salaries*
Low	95.3
Lower middle	91.0
Upper middle	87.9
High	76.1

Source: Lockheed and Verspoor (forthcoming).

Table A-8. New Teachers Required to Achieve 100 Percent Gross Enrollment in Year 2000
(thousands)

Country income level	*Estimated population age 6-11 in 2000*	*Teaching force in 1985*	*Additional teachers needed*	*Teachers lost through attrition, 1985–2000*	*Additional teachers needed (adjusted for attrition)*
Low[a]	154,448	1,727	2,238	1,076	3,314
China and India	268,314	7,244	1,091	3,473	4,564
Lower middle	136,570	3,543	878	1,756	2,634
Upper middle	118,335	3,778	178	1,725	1,903

Note: Data assume existing child population growth rates, current student-teacher ratios, and nominal 3 percent teacher attrition rates.

a. Excluding China and India.

Source: Lockheed and Verspoor (forthcoming).

Table A-9. Population, School Places, and Enrollments for Ninety-nine Developing Countries, 1985

Country income level	*Population age 6–11 (millions)*	*Primary school places (millions)*	*Children age 6–11 enrolled (millions)*	*Children age 6–11 out of school*		*"Excess" places[a] (millions)*	*Out-of-school children for whom places are available (percent)*
				(millions)	*(percent)*		
Low[b]	104.7	66.6	54.0	50.7	48.5	12.6	24.8
China and India[c]	235.4	220.2	174.3	61.1	26.0	45.9	75.1
Lower middle	104.9	104.4	83.6	21.3	20.3	20.8	97.7
Upper middle	81.8	91.1	69.5	12.3	15.0	21.6	175.9
Total	526.8	482.3	381.5	145.3	27.6	100.8	69.4

a. The number of primary school places minus the number of children age six to eleven enrolled.

b. Excluding China and India.

c. These figures do not take into account the fact that six-year-olds in China are not expected to be in school.

Source: Lockheed and Verspoor (forthcoming).

Table A-10. Summary of Cost Effects of Specific Recommendations

Input	Reduce costs	No change	Increase costs: Investment	Increase costs: Recurrent
Inputs that raise learning				
Improved curriculum[a]	—	—	✓	—
Textbooks and materials	—	—	✓	✓
Minimum instructional time	—	✓	—	—
On-site in-service teacher training	—	—	—	✓
Interactive radio instruction	—	—	✓	—
Programmed materials	—	—	✓	—
Micronutrients and health interventions	—	—	—	✓
School snacks	—	—	—	✓
Teacher training reform[b]	✓[c]	—	—	✓[c]
Inputs that have no negative effect on learning				
Multigrade classes	✓	—	—	—
Multiple shifts	✓	—	—	—
Low-cost school construction	✓	—	—	—
Class size of 40–50 students	✓[d]	—	—	✓[d]
Parental outreach program	—	—	—	✓
Reduction of discriminatory practices	—	—	—	✓[e]
Private provision of schooling	✓	—	—	—
Inputs that improve management				
Career ladders for teachers and managers	—	—	—	✓
Salary/nonsalary[f] incentives for teachers	—	—	✓	✓
Rationalized management structures	—	✓	—	—
Information systems	—	—	✓	✓
Staff training	—	—	—	✓

Note: A check mark (✓) indicates where effect is felt.

a. Correct scope and sequence.

b. Raise pretraining general education requirements and shorten preservice training.

c. Teacher training costs will be reduced; salary costs will increase.

d. Costs will be reduced where classes are smaller than 40–50 students; costs will increase where classes are larger than 40–50 students.

e. Training and supervision costs will increase.

f. For example, housing in rural areas.

Table A-11. Median Public Expenditures on Education as a Percentage of GNP, in Selected Years, 1965–85

Country income level	*1965*	*1970*	*1975*	*1980*	*1985*
Low	2.7	3.2	2.8	3.1	3.2
Lower middle	3.0	3.4	3.6	4.5	3.9
Upper middle	3.2	3.4	3.5	3.7	4.3
High	4.3	5.1	6.3	5.8	5.8

Source: Lockheed and Verspoor (forthcoming).

Table A-12. Median Public Recurrent Expenditure Per Primary Pupil, in Selected Years, 1965–85
(1985 dollars)

Country income level	*1965*	*1970*	*1975*	*1980*	*1985*
Low	40.7	38.7	40.7	29.4	30.9
Lower middle	72.5	71.3	81.6	75.5	101.7
Upper middle	194.3	197.9	258.9	255.7	296.6
High	824.5	841.7	1,117.6	1,382.8	1,551.4
Ratio of low-income country spending to high-income country spending	1:20	1:22	1:27	1:47	1:50

Source: Lockheed and Verspoor (forthcoming).

Table A-13. Median Public Recurrent Expenditure Per Primary Pupil, as a Percentage of GNP per Capita, in Selected Years, 1965–85

Country income level	*1965*	*1970*	*1975*	*1980*	*1985*
Low	20.0	14.0	13.0	11.7	11.9
Lower middle	10.3	11.0	9.2	9.5	10.9
Upper middle	10.6	8.9	8.1	9.1	12.5
High	11.7	11.5	14.4	15.9	17.6

Source: Lockheed and Verspoor (forthcoming).

Table A-14. Student-Teacher Ratios in 116 Countries, 1985
(percentage of countries)

Country income level	*Less than 40:1*	*40–50:1*	*More than 50:1*
Low	54	23	23
Lower middle	79	15	6
Upper middle	96	4	0
High	100	0	0

Source: Computed from Lockheed and Verspoor (forthcoming).

Table A-15. Change in Public Recurrent Expenditure If Student-Teacher Ratio Is Altered
(percent)

		Savings gained (expense incurred)	
Country income level	*Student-teacher ratio in 1985*	*If ratio increases (decreases) to 40:1*	*If ratio increases (decreases) to 45:1*
Low (median)	42	(4.70)	6.06
Bangladesh	47	(9.41)	(2.37)
Burkina Faso	62	(52.10)	(35.67)
Burundi	56	(39.30)	(23.98)
Central African Republic	66	(63.47)	(45.55)
China	25	33.04	39.08
Ethiopia	48	(17.72)	(6.04)
Ghana	23	37.05	42.64
Guinea	36	8.04	16.85
Haiti	38	4.14	11.43
India	46	(13.76)	(2.52)
Kenya	34	13.16	21.40
Lesotho	52	(30.80)	(16.28)
Madagascar	38	4.96	15.47
Malawi	61	(48.57)	(33.01
Mali	34	14.86	24.13
Mauritania	51	(22.61)	(10.40)
Nepal	35	8.72	16.28
Pakistan	40	(0.01)	9.69
Sudan	35	11.59	20.01
Tanzania	34	8.39	13.92
Togo	46	(15.47)	(2.84)
Zambia	49	(21.01)	(8.72)
Lower middle (median)	31	17.94	25.92
Upper middle (median)	25	31.21	37.40

Source: Computed from Lockheed and Verspoor (forthcoming).

Table A-16. Community Support for Primary Schools, Zambia, 1979–84

Type of support	*Percentage of schools receiving support*
Service on school committees	58.7
Building materials	52.2
Skilled and unskilled labor	50.0
Voluntary cash	43.5
Compulsory cash levies	41.2
Building plans	21.7
Land	17.4
Lodging facilities for boarders	17.4
Meals for pupils	2.2

Source: Kaluba in Bray and Lillis (1988).

Table A-17. Distribution of Aid to Primary Education, 1981–86
(percent)

Type of aid	*All countries*	*Low-income countries*	*Lower middle-income countries*	*Upper middle-income countries*
Books and instructional materials	4.8	7.5	3.9	0.8
Furniture and equipment	6.3	16.2	2.6	1.0
Technical assistance	14.0	17.6	13.1	0.9
Food/scholarships	15.3	20.7	14.3	0.7
Buildings	23.4	22.1	25.8	3.3
Budgetary assistance	29.9	5.7	34.8	90.3
Other	6.3	10.2	5.6	3.0

Source: IREDU (1989).

Table A-18. World Bank Lending Commitments for Primary Education, Fiscal 1963–89

Fiscal year	*Lending for primary education (millions of dollars[a])*	*Total education lending (millions of dollars[a])*	*Primary education as percentage of total education lending*
1963–69	0.0	243.9	0.0
1970–74	36.5	814.9	4.5
1975–80	300.8	2,121.7	14.2
1981–85	776.6	3,460.9	22.4
1986–89	862.9	3,107.3	27.8

a. Current dollars.
Source: World Bank data.

Bibliography

The word "processed" describes works that are reproduced from typescript by mimeograph, xerography, or similar means; such works may not be cataloged or commonly available through libraries, or they may be subject to restricted circulation.

Anderson, Mary B. 1988. *Improving Access to Schooling in the Third World: An Overview.* BRIDGES Research Report Series, Issue 1. Cambridge, Mass.: Harvard University.

Benavot, Aaron. Forthcoming. *Education and Economic Development in the Modern World.* Oxford: Pergamon Press.

Benavot, Aaron, and David Kamens. 1989. "The Curricular Content of Primary Education in Developing Countries." Policy, Planning, and Research Working Paper 237. World Bank, Population and Human Resources Department, Washington, D.C. Processed.

Boissiere, M., John B. Knight, and Richard H. Sabot. 1985. "Earnings, Schooling, Ability and Cognitive Skills." *American Economic Review* 75 (5): 1016–30.

Bray, Mark, and Kevin Lillis. 1988. *Community Financing of Education: Issues and Policy Implications in Less Developed Countries.* Oxford: Pergamon Press.

Chesterfield, Ray, and H. Ned Seelye. 1986. *Process Evaluation of the Programa Nacional de Educacion Bilingue* (PRONEBI). Final Report for USAID/Guatemala and PRONEBI. Washington, D.C.: United States Agency for International Development.

Cochrane, Susan H. 1986. "The Effects of Education on Fertility and Mortality." Education and Training Department Discussion Paper 26. World Bank, Population and Human Resources Department, Washington, D.C. Processed.

Eisemon, Thomas O. 1988. *Benefiting from Basic Education, School Quality and Functional Literacy in Kenya.* Oxford: Pergamon Press.

Elley, W. B., and Francis Mangubhai. 1983. "The Impact of Reading on Second Language Learning." *Reading Research Quarterly* 19 (1): 53–67.

Farrell, Joseph P., and Stephen P. Heyneman, eds. 1989. *Textbooks in the Developing World: Economic and Educational Choices.* Washington, D.C.: World Bank.

Fuller, Bruce. 1987. "Raising School Quality in Developing Countries: What Investments Boost Learning." *Review of Educational Research* 57 (3): 255–92.

Gimenos, José B., and Ricardo M. Ibanez. 1981. *The Education of Primary and Secondary School Teachers: An International Comparative Study*. Paris: Unesco (United Nations Educational, Scientific and Cultural Organization).

Halpern, Robert, and Robert Myers. 1985. *Effects of Early Childhood Intervention on Primary School Progress and Performance in the Developing Countries*. Washington, D.C.: United States Agency for International Development.

Hanson, Mark E. 1986. *Education Reform and Administrative Development: The Cases of Colombia and Venezuela*. Stanford, Calif.: Hoover Institution Press.

Harbison, Ralph W., and Eric Hanushek. Forthcoming. *Educational Performance of the Poor: Lessons from Rural Northeast Brazil*. Washington, D.C.: World Bank.

Haverman, Robert H., and Barbara L. Wolfe. 1984. "Schooling and Economic Well-being: The Role of Non-market Effects." *Journal of Human Resources* 19 (3): 377–406.

Horn, Robin, and Ana-Maria Arriagada. 1986. "The Educational Attainment of the World's Population: Three Decades of Progress." Education and Training Department Discussion Paper 37. World Bank, Population and Human Resources Department, Washington, D.C. Processed.

Huberman, A. Michael, and Matthew B. Miles. 1984. *Innovation Up Close: How School Improvement Works*. New York: Plenum Press.

IEA (International Association for the Evaluation of Educational Achievement). 1988. *Science Achievement in Seventeen Countries: A Preliminary Report*. Oxford: Pergamon Press.

ILO (International Labour Office). 1988. *Yearbook of Labour Statistics*. Geneva.

IREDU (Institut de Recherche sur l'Economie de l'Education). 1989. "External Aid for Primary Education in Developing Countries." Dijon: University of Bourgogne. Processed.

Jimenez, Emmanuel. 1987. *Pricing Policy in the Social Sectors: Cost Recovery for Education and Health in Developing Countries*. Baltimore, Md.: Johns Hopkins University Press.

King, Elizabeth M., and Anne Hill, eds. Forthcoming. "Determinants and Consequences of Educating Women in the Third World." Book draft. World Bank, Population and Human Resources Department, Washington, D.C. Processed.

Komenan, André. 1987. "World Education Indicators." Education and Training Department Discussion Paper 88. World Bank, Population and Human Resources Department, Washington, D.C. Processed.

Levin, Henry M., Gene V. Glass, and Gail Meister. 1984. *Cost Effectiveness of Four Educational Interventions*. Stanford, Calif.: Institute for Research on Education Finance and Governance.

Lockheed, Marlaine E., Dean T. Jamison, and Lawrence Lau. 1980. "Farmer Education and Farm Efficiency: A Survey." *Economic Development and Cultural Change* 29 (1): 37–76.

Lockheed, Marlaine E., and Eric Hanushek. 1988. "Improving Educational Efficiency in Developing Countries: What Do We Know?" *Compare*. 18 (1): 21–38.

Lockheed, Marlaine E., John Middleton, and Greta Nettleton, eds. Forthcoming. *Technology and Teaching: Elements of Sustainability in Developing Countries*. Washington, D.C.: World Bank.

Lockheed, Marlaine E., and Adriaan M. Verspoor, with Deborah Bloch, Pierre Englebert, Bruce Fuller, Elizabeth King, John Middleton, Vicente Paqueo, Alastair

Rodd, Ralph Romain, and Michel Welmond. Forthcoming. *Improving Primary Education in Developing Countries.* New York: Oxford University Press.

O'Connor, Sorca. 1988. "Women's Labor Force Participation and Preschool Enrollment: A Cross-national Perspective, 1965–1980." *Sociology of Education* 61 (1): 15–28.

Oliveira, Joao B., and François Orivel. 1981. "Cost Effectiveness Analysis of an In-service Teacher Training System: Logos II in Brazil." Population and Human Resources Division Discussion Paper 81-40. World Bank, Population and Human Resources Department, Washington, D.C. Processed.

Pollitt, Ernesto. 1990. *Malnutrition and Infection in the Classroom.* Paris: Unesco (United Nations Educational, Scientific and Cultural Organization).

Psacharopoulos, George. 1985. "Returns to Education: A Further International Update and Implications." *Journal of Human Resources* 20 (4): 584–604.

Psacharopoulos, George, Jee-Peng Tan, and Emmanuel Jimenez. 1986. *Financing Education in Developing Countries. An Exploration of Policy Options.* Washington, D.C.: World Bank.

Psacharopoulos, George, and Maureen Woodhall. 1985. *Education for Development: Analysis of Investment Choices.* New York: Oxford University Press.

Purkey, Stewart L., and Marshall S. Smith. 1983. "Effective Schools: A Review." *The Elementary School Journal.* 83 (4): 427–52.

Resnick, Lauren B. 1987. *Education and Learning to Think.* Washington, D.C.: National Academy Press.

Rondinelli, Dennis, John Middleton, and Adriaan Verspoor. 1989. *Planning Education Reforms in Developing Countries: A Contingency Approach.* Durham, N.C.: Duke University Press.

Rust, Val D., and Per Dalin, eds. 1990. *Teachers and Teaching in the Developing World.* New York: Garland Press.

Schultz, T. Paul. 1985. "School Expenditure and Enrollments, 1960–1980: The Effect of Income, Prices and Population Growth." Yale University, Economic Growth Center Discussion Paper 487. New Haven, Conn. Processed.

Taylor, D. C. 1983. "The Cost-Effectiveness of Teacher Upgrading by Distance Teaching in Southern Africa." *International Journal of Educational Development* 3 (1): 19–31.

Thailand, Ministry of Education. 1987. *National Evaluation Results for Sixth Grade Students.* Office of the National Primary Education Commission, Bangkok.

Unesco (United Nations Educational, Scientific and Cultural Organization). 1989. *Statistical Yearbook 1989.* Paris.

Verspoor, Adriaan. 1989. *Pathways to Change: Improving the Quality of Education in Developing Countries.* World Bank Discussion Paper 53. Washington, D.C.

Wheeler, Christopher W., Stephen Raudenbush, Pragob Kunarak, and Aida Pasigna. 1989. *Policy Initiatives to Improve School Quality in Thailand: An Essay on Implementation, Constraints, and Opportunity for Educational Improvement.* BRIDGES Research Report Series, Issue 5. Cambridge, Mass.: Harvard University.

Winkler, Donald R. 1989. "Decentralization in Education: An Economic Perspective." Policy, Planning, and Research Working Paper 143. World Bank, Population and Human Resources Department, Washington, D.C. Processed.

World Bank. 1988. *World Development Report 1988.* New York: Oxford University Press.

Zymelman, Manuel, and Joseph DeStefano. 1989. *Primary School Teachers' Salaries in Sub-Saharan Africa.* World Bank Discussion Paper 45. Washington, D.C.